EARLY AVIATION

IN PORTER COUNTY, INDIANA

CINDA URSCHEL

Table of Contents

Dedication

This book is dedicated to Patricia McMahon, as it would never have come to fruition without her invaluable advice, assistance, and support. Her innumerable hours of editing and research are so greatly appreciated. Her joy and keen interest kept me going, enabling me to finish the book.

I would like to thank all the pilots who were interviewed. Without Nena Winder Babcock's initial meeting, I would not have started this project.

And lastly, a big thank-you to my family and friends who gave me much encouragement and support along the way.

Preface
Serendipity

Nena Winder and I first met at Urschel Laboratories while employees were filming interviews of World War II veterans for a Porter County Museum project. Nena was there to talk about her husband Owen's (Bus) wartime experiences. I was there filming a segment on Women Airforce Service Pilots (WASP).

While discussing Porter County WASP Bette Nogard Richards, Nena told me she knew Bette and had several photos of them together in the 1930s. My perception of Bette being the first woman licensed pilot in Porter County was refuted. The first licensed woman pilot in Porter County was none other than Nena herself.

At Nena's home a few days after our initial introduction, we continued the discussion of early Porter County aviation and Nena's recollections of Urschel Field. While there, my eyes fell on a beautiful farmhouse painting. Surprisingly, I felt a very strong attraction to this farmhouse, which normally would not have caught my attention. Nena informed me it was a painting of my grandfather William Urschel's house on his farm adjacent to Urschel Field. I was just stunned. Nena and her family had lived in the farmhouse, as did other pilots in the early days. I requested that Nena contact her old friend Harriet Rex Smith to find out when she painted it and if she had any photographs of it.

I later talked with Harriet, who lives in Oregon and still paints. She permitted me to make a giclée print of this painting. She said she sat in front of the farmhouse one day and painted it, probably sometime in the late 1930s or early 1940s.

So began my journey to gather stories from the aviation legends who were still living, research the others who had offered so much, including sometimes their life, to further aviation in Porter County, and share the stories with anyone who has an inclination to honor these curious, intelligent, farsighted individuals. Ready to take off with me?

Porter County Townships

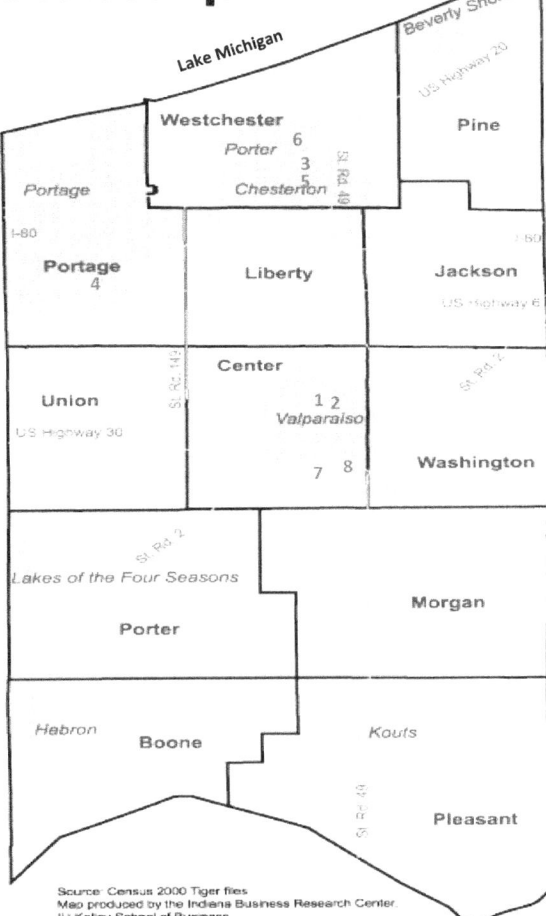

Porter County Airports

1. Urschel Field
2. C. Lee Nelson Field
3. Chesterton Airport
4. McCool Airport
5. DeMass Farm
6. Bodin Airport
7. Oakley Lutes Field
8. Bud Winder Field

Source: Census 2000 Tiger files
Map produced by the Indiana Business Research Center,
IU Kelley School of Business

William Emmet Urschel
April 6, 1880–September 7, 1948

Ruth Richards Urschel
November 29, 1883–April 5, 1975

My grandfather William had many passions in his life. He was an artist, a gold miner in Idaho, a deputy postmaster in Pierce, Idaho, an original government surveyor for the Bitter Root Mountains between Montana and Idaho, and an inventor.

He graduated from the School of Fine Arts at Valparaiso College in 1901. He then spent two years in Idaho after he filed for a homestead land grant in Idaho's white pine timber belt. He felled the timber and built a log cabin. William and his friend John Collins decided to mine for gold. They struck gold, but the ore fizzled out at about 25 feet, rendering it insignificant.

During a snowy winter in Idaho, the idea struck William that he could invent a machine that could snip the stems and blossoms from gooseberries that his father grew back on the family farm in Indiana. In 1904 he sold his interest in the mine and returned to Valparaiso, Indiana, to take a postgraduate course in the fine arts. In a barn near Valparaiso University, he worked hard on his design, and students nicknamed him "Gooseberry Bill." Running low on funds, he lived in Chicago for two years, designing hand-painted china at Lakeside Studio, which was part of White's Art Company. A large group of employees at this business then hand painted his designs. While in Chicago, he completed postgraduate work at The Art Institute of Chicago, receiving his Master of Fine Arts degree. In 1907 he came back to Valparaiso to begin designing the Gooseberry Snipper. He filed for his first of many patents on June 22, 1908.

In August 1910 Ruth and William married, and that year he established The Gooseberry Snipper Factory. They built the machines in a little

1

shop next to their kitchen at 158 South Napoleon Street in Valparaiso. My grandmother even ran a lathe and helped him in all aspects of the new business.

In the 1937 book *The Canning Clan*, by Earl Chapin May, William is featured in the chapter entitled "Great Machines From Little Snippers Grow."

Flying was a lifelong passion of William's starting in eighth grade while he was living in Manchester, Indiana. He drew plans and made models of airplanes. He needed $4,000 to build a plane, so it was not built. This was a few years before the Wright brothers invented their plane. William and friends Vaughn Harvil and Glen J. Goddard dreamed of an airfield for Valparaiso. They had planned on purchasing a Swallow plane made in Wichita, Kansas, and having it brought to Valparaiso for inspection; however, that plane was never purchased.

William established Urschel Field because he felt aviation would promote growth and success in this area of Indiana. The airport site was the A. V. and Emma Bartholomew farm of 1876. The property had been divided in 1906, giving the land south of Vale Park Road to R. Bartholomew, while W. Bartholomew owned the land north of Vale Park Road. As of 1921 Fred and Pauline Tresemer owned the land north of Vale Park Road.

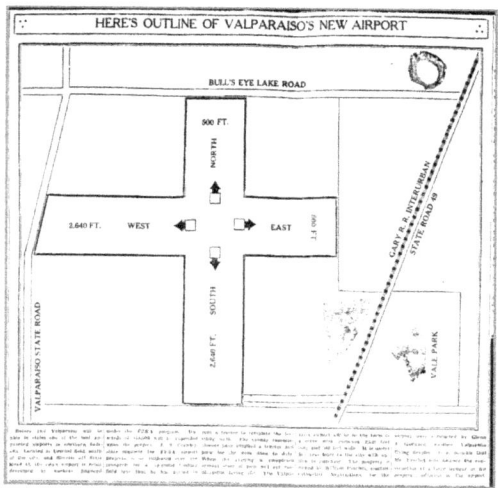

Larry Clark, historian at the Valparaiso branch of the Porter County Library, said records show that in 1926 William owned 168 acres bounded by Bullseye Lake Road on the north, Calumet Avenue (State Road 49) on the east, Vale Park Road to the south, and Valparaiso Street to the west. Originally William had intended to subdivide this parcel for business purposes. A small triangular strip of land next to Calumet Avenue was owned by James and E. Dye at one time.

William also acquired 87 acres in the northeast Section 13 in 1928. This was south of Vale Park Road and extended down to Glendale Road.

On June 16, 1929, to help promote aviation, William drove to Goshen, Indiana, along with other community-minded aviation enthusiasts, to board a Ford Tri-Motor all-metal plane piloted by Ray Loomis. Some of the other passengers were Mayor Louis Leetz, J. William Bosse, T. L. Applegate, Harry Arnold, and H. M. Evans. They were flying back to Urschel Field, where hundreds of people who had purchased $5 tickets for a 25-minute ride were waiting. The pilot had delayed leaving Goshen due to heavy rain. They finally took off on the 75-mile trip that would take them 50 minutes. When the plane landed at Urschel Field, it became mired in mud and could not be flown out, disappointing those waiting. The ticket holders were told they could get their money refunded or drive 30 miles to Knox, Indiana, the next day for a ride.

When interviewed in *The Vidette-Messenger*, William described the trip as follows:

> The flight from Goshen to Valparaiso was my first cross-country trip in the air. During the first 15 minutes of the flight, everyone seemed very excited about the wonders visible below. Gradually we became quiet. The little threads representing railroads, highways, and the like did not interest me so much as the many colors of soil in different fields. Some freshly plowed fields containing both high and low ground represented artistic design. I felt no uneasiness until we passed Wanatah; from there on many fields were flooded with water, and I began to wonder whether or not we would take a nosedive when landing. My uneasiness ceased when we came to a stop right side up. I certainly enjoyed the trip and feel that the large Ford plane affords safe transportation. Before another year has passed, I hope to make business trips across the country via airplane.[1]

In 1931 a government aviation official selected the land at Urschel Field to be one of two best sites for an airfield. On January 2, 1934, the city council passed the ordinance for Valparaiso to lease from William

---

1. "Rain-Soaked Field Foils Flying Event," *Vidette-Messenger*, June 17, 1929.

for five years 60 acres of his land for Urschel Field to become a municipal airport. At any time the city could purchase this land at $225 per acre. The first year of the lease was $50, the second was $250, and the third through the fifth years would be $350.

In 1934 under a $14,000 grant from the Civil Works Administration (CWA), the airport was improved. In August 1934 Federal Emergency Relief Administration (FERA) workers placed drain tiles and scraped the two runways; when this was finished, they seeded the runway.

In 1935 William wanted the city to give the airport 70,000 to 80,000 Lincolnway paving bricks to build a hangar to house 12 planes in exchange for what the city owed in its lease agreement. The discussions dragged on for months, and one councilman believed the citizens of Valparaiso were concerned about the value of an airport. In the end the city declined William's request.

In early 1936 the Bureau of Aeronautics stated that no more government monies would be spent to upgrade Urschel Field. A $47,000 grant was contingent on the city owning the land and Urschel Field becoming an official municipal airport. William and other pilots tried working with the city. In December 1936 William and 20 members of the Aero Club met with the city council, demanding the city make up its mind: Break the lease, or keep going with plans to obtain federal money to finish the airport. The lease was canceled in January 1937 when the council did not want to expend any more money for the airport.

Urschel Field returned to being a private airport even though almost all cities had municipal airports during this time. Bud Winder took over as manager. William built the first hangar in 1938, followed by the second, larger hangar in 1941. The pilots loved him for he was instrumental in building Urschel Field. He gave Bud Winder the support necessary to operate the airport and always maintained an active interest in the field's operations as shown by his frequent visits to the airport as he enjoyed watching all of the activity taking place there.

During their observation of Aviation Day in December 1938, which was the 35th anniversary of the Wrights' Kitty Hawk flight, Valparaiso Aero Club members honored William and Bud for supporting the club since its inception. More than 150 aviation enthusiasts joined in this celebration.

FLY
40ᶜ
Tomorrow
and
Sunday
Urschel Airport
Giant 4½-ton
Airliner

RATES
SATURDAY
2:30 to 3 P. M. .. 40c
3 to Dark 50c

SUNDAY
10 A. M. to 10:30 . 40c
10:30 to Dark ... 50c

In 1944 the city was listed to receive an award of $305,000 from the Civil Aeronautics Administration (CAA) in Washington to use for an airport. Of these monies, $80,000 was for preparation of the field, $210,000 for paving the runways, $12,000 for lighting, $1,000 for radio equipment, and the remaining for miscellaneous purposes. Engineers from the Economic Council surveyed possible airport sites. John J. Hogan, a district engineer of the CAA, stated that Valparaiso was included in the CAA's national list of airport facilities and the building of new fields. Their recommendation on whether Urschel Field could use these monies or if they would go toward the construction of a new field was kept under wraps. The decision did not favor Urschel Field.

In July 1945 William took his first long air trip. Olie Sundelin flew him to Columbus, Ohio, in a Stinson. The trip took 2 hours and 20 minutes. He took the fastest train back to Valparaiso, which took 9 hours.

In 1947 William spoke at the annual Aviation Day banquet of the Valparaiso Aero Club at Bloch's Hotel. More than 150 flyers and aviation enthusiasts from the area attended.

William passed away on September 7, 1948, after a two-year illness. In the 1950s Urschel Field was reported by several of the people I interviewed to be the busiest private airport in the country, a fact which would have pleased and amazed him. A few months after his death, Urschel Field was awarded the National Aeronautics Association Certificate for good airport-operating practices. William's wife Ruth told her sons Joe, Gerald, and Kenneth that the airport would be kept open for she knew her husband had been passionate about it.

Porter County Airport was established in 1949 east of State Road 49 and north of U.S. Route 30. At the 1950 airport grand opening, William was honored with a tribute for being one of the county's foremost aviation pioneers. Porter County Airport was dedicated in the spring of 1951.

On February 28, 1961, the north hangar at Urschel Field burned to the ground, and two planes were destroyed. Several other planes were pulled to safety. By April 1962 Willard Rusk, who was managing Urschel

Field, had moved most of his operation to Kankakee, Illinois. Willard left Charles Younce in charge of his business at Urschel Field to fulfill jobs such as crop dusting, instructing students, and running the repair shop.

Late in 1963 Urschel Field closed, and large Xs were dug into the runways. Most pilots and mechanics had moved to either Porter County Airport or Kankakee Airport. Willard removed the last piece of equipment from Urschel Field on July 1, 1964. What a great airport it had been for 30 years!

William's son Joe (my father) started taking flying lessons on September 17, 1936, in a Waco 10 OX-5 and soloed on September 22, 1936. He also had training in a Taylor Cub. Joe's instructors were Bud Winder, Ralph Barneko, Henry Foster, and Bob Lenburg. The last entry in Joe's logbook was February 5, 1939. Most of the pages in his logbook showed him practicing landing. He had poor depth perception and never received his private pilot's license. Joe participated in a 1938 air show flying through toilet paper that he had flung out the window. He still went flying, even without a license.

Gladys Swain Urschel, Joe's wife, was the first woman to fly solo in Michigan City, Indiana, on November 5, 1941, in a Piper Cub. She did this at age twenty-eight during her lunch hour. Her first lesson was on

Gladys age 28

September 6, 1941, in a J-3 Cub. Her last entry in her logbook was December 7, 1941, when many airports were closed for a while due to the war.

Joe and Gladys always instilled in their children (Bill, Dan, Elena, Janet, Bob, and me) how very dangerous it was to fly small "death trap" aircraft. Many kids developed their love of flying by hanging out at the airport; however, we were warned not to go there because of the danger it posed. They scared us enough with all their comments that none of us desired to fly at that time.

My daughter Heather Lynch decided in 2001 that she wanted to learn to fly. She started ground school and was undeterred by all the negative comments made by family members. She took her first flying lesson at Porter County Airport on June 23, 2001, in a Piper Cub with Guy Campolattara as her instructor. She took only one lesson after that. Her decision to quit was not from fear but due to other plans in her life.

Rick Urschel, Bob's son, at age eight, had the opportunity to taxi around Porter County Airport in a Stearman. His mother would not allow him to fly at such a young age. It must have planted a seed, as he took a discovery flight 17 years later on August 8, 2003. He soloed on September 5, 2003, in a Cessna 172 Skyhawk, receiving his private pilot's certificate on November 13, 2004, and his instrument rating on July 28, 2005. He had done much of this without his parents knowing what he had done. After finally divulging to his parents what he had been doing, they were not too happy. His father Bob finally allowed his son to take him up, and they flew along the shore of Lake Michigan. Well, Bob was hooked and started taking lessons a few weeks later.

Bob had his first discovery flight on August 15, 2005, and his first solo flight on November 2, 2005, in a C-172 Skyhawk. He received his private pilot's license on February 19, 2006, and his instrument rating on November 3, 2006, in a Cirrus SR22. He also earned the following: Commercial Pilot, Certified Flight Instructor, Instrument (CFI & CFIII), and Airline Transport Pilot (ATP) certifications.

Father and son are both excellent pilots. They have owned a Cirrus SR22, a Pilatus PC-12, a TBM 850, and a Cirrus Vision Jet SF50.

Yes, you might say that these Urschels received the aviation gene from Grandpa William although he never did pilot a plane. More importantly, thousands of men and women could enjoy the beauty and the promise of flight from their flying escapades at Urschel Field. I can only imagine the satisfaction William experienced knowing he played an integral part in advocating and advancing aviation when it was in its infancy. And for that, we are most thankful!

Dr. Arthur Van Winkle

April 30, 1887–January 20, 1957

The physician for our pilots and their families! Early Porter County aviators were very fortunate to have Dr. Van Winkle's expertise not only in delivering their babies, such as Dixie Lee Winder, but also in administering the medical exams required by the U.S. Department of Commerce to obtain and keep their pilot's licenses. One of the tests was for depth perception. He had two strings about 20 feet long. Each string had a pin. The doctor would pull them apart, and then the patient pulled on one of the strings and had to line them up. Dr. Van Winkle started flying in 1918 and joined the Aero Club in 1936.[2] He had a strong bond with this community of flyers. He wrote a column on aviation for *The Vidette-Messenger*. Ray Miller remarked that Dr. Van Winkle, who came to the airport frequently, was a funny man who was always a pleasure to be around. The doctor himself owned a J-3 Cub and then a three-passenger Stinson, requiring the person in the back to sit sideways.

In June 1950 he represented Porter County at the International Aero-Medical Society's annual scientific meeting in Chicago.[3] Representatives from many countries studied the problems of aviation pilots and passengers through research. In 1950 the society had 6,000 members and offered 37 fellowships. Dr. Van Winkle was awarded one of those fellowships, which was a special honor.

In 1953 he traveled by plane to Honolulu to address that same group. The 1955 scientific meeting was in Washington, DC, with more than 10,000 physicians attending. The theme of that convention was "Safety for the Ordinary Pilot."[4]

2. "Two Local Flying Doctors Procure Stinson Planes," *Vidette-Messenger*, June 13, 1950.
3. "Doctor Attends Aero-Medical Meeting," *Vidette-Messenger*, June 1, 1950.
4. "Doctor Returns from Convention in U.S. Capital," *Vidette-Messenger*, March 2, 1955.

URSCHEL·FIELD·VALPARAISO·IND.

By A. J. VAN WINKLE
Why?

Why do pilots get that way? Why are they so unselfish and kindly to each other, and so helpful to hte pilot in trouble? Why are they most always pretty happy and hopeful? Why do they take good care of even their autos and things? Why are they always craving for each other's company? Why do they hurt inside when another pilot is injured whether whether they know him or not? I don't know, I'm asking you.

Good Luck and God Bless You

Today leaves for Oakland, Calif., one Major John L. Winder, (Bud to you) and for Charlotte, S. C., one Henry S. Foster. Both of these pilots have worked hard to get where they are. Both are now engaged in hard, hazardous work. Precise, alert, resourceful, energetic, controlled, cheerful, frank, enthusiastic, with good sportsmanship are just a few adjectives that poorly describe the good pilot of today. They are both excellent pilots. We have welcomed them into our homes for they have always been in our hearts. There have been many parties. There they talked of flying and of planes; of God and of the "why" of it all. We just don't understand those that move in the third dimension. Maybe that is why we love them. (Strange to speak of it, but pilots have the utmost respect for the submarine crew.) As for me, give me the aid, Bud Winder, Henry Foster, Bill Younce, Al Parsons, Claude Lendburg, Gunnard Nielsen, Bun Blackman, Oile Sundelin, Rollie Humphrey were to nearly every party. Later on, when we have brought to their knees the Nipponese, we will be having the annual banquet. We will eat turkey and steak and fish, and crab about the service. But and Hank —we have so enjoyed your visit. Maybe the next time old Axe Nogard and Bob Ulsh and Lawrence Gesse and others will be there too. Good luck and God bless you.

Thermals

Rollie Humphrey has bought out Soetje and Hern of LaPorte Airport. Will have four or more A. and E. Mechanics for the heavy backlog of repair; will buy and sell airplanes and parts. He has a fine location and will do well. Remember when you used to buy things of him at Lowenstines'? The secret of his success is hard work, careful care of his body and a sincere good will for every one. That stuff works in any business ...Reggie Pendelton has a hangar next door and has his instructor's rating. Has a converted Laison T-craft that flies mighty sweet...Rollie and Reggie, you have the idea ...All pilots are agin' the new rules by Wright and Henry Wallace. If you own airplane stock it may pay you for the first year. But it will cost so many human lives that it ain't funny McGee. The new autos will take a tremendous toll of lives and health. We pilots don't want that in the air. We are a different bunch of screwballs. And so, in spite of a couple of dippy officials, let us choose with care our plane, fly with care that plane. Fly it fast for safety, and be afraid.

(EDITOR'S NOTE — Appearing for the first time in print, is the new cut, above, for Urschel Field Flying Notes. It was made from a pen and ink sketch of the field by William Urschel, flying enthusiast, inventor and owner of Urschel Laboratories. Hereafter it will head the weekly column of local flying notes in this newspaper.)

9

James (Jack) Brockett Knight
March 14, 1892–February 24, 1945

After his mom died Jack was adopted by Dr. and Mrs. Melvin Knight, his aunt and uncle from Buchanan, Michigan.[5] In 1910 he enrolled at Michigan Agricultural College (Michigan State) as a mechanical engineering student. Jack was known to play pranks and was later suspended when the pranks became problematic.

Before World War I, Jack was a draftsman and engineer at Mead-Morrison Engineering Corporation in Chicago. Jack began flying in 1916, and the following year he joined the U.S. Army Air Service as a pilot. He was so good they made him an instructor at Ellington Field in Houston, Texas.

After the war he returned to his Chicago engineering job. One day the members of his squadron were in Chicago and did a dogfight in the airspace above the building where he worked. He watched their antics from the roof. "I got so excited I went downstairs and quit, wired Washington, DC, and got on as a mail pilot."[6]

Mail was flown from San Francisco to New York in 78 hours. The train took about the same time as flying and was cheaper. Congress wanted to discontinue the airmail service and use only trains. On February 22-23, 1921, Knight and a group of aviators wanted to prove to Congress they could do this faster, and they decided to fly the mail part of the time at night. The seven-member team flew 2,629 miles in 33 hours and 20 minutes. Only 26 hours of that time was spent in the air. This was very dangerous, because the pilots had only huge bonfires

5. Debra Haight, "Famed Buchanan Pilot to Be Featured in Local History Programs," Leader Publications, May 24, 2022, https://www.leaderpub.com/2022/05/24/famed-buchanan-pilot-to-be-featured-in-local-history-programs/.
6. Steve Fisher, "Knight Flyer," Historynet, February 4, 2020, https://www.historynet.com/knight-flier/.

to guide them on their routes and the landing fields were rough. Jack's portion of this relay team was to fly from Cheyenne, Wyoming, to Omaha, Nebraska, but when he landed in Nebraska, the relief pilot was nowhere to be found. The relief pilot was stuck in Chicago in a snowstorm. Jack decided to continue to Chicago in his open cockpit. When he hit Des Moines, the ceiling was 400 feet, and all the bonfires were out because it was a complete blizzard. He had never flown this leg and had to navigate from town to town with very strong headwinds using only a compass and a torn road map. He flew on to Iowa City, where a night watchman heard his plane and ran out onto the field with two railroad flares to aid Jack's landing. The temperature was a bitter -12 degrees. He left the plane running, ate, refueled, and took off for Chicago. He flew a total of 830 miles. He said the flight was brutal due to the temperature, a broken nose, frozen wind, and bumpy air. The week before his historic flight, he had broken his nose in a crash in a de Havilland DH-48 mail plane. Impressed by what the team had done, Congress decided to appropriate the funds for the airmail service. On July 1, 1924, airmail became regularly scheduled and was a 24-hour operation. The cost of airmail postage was 8 cents an ounce.

Jack became a household name and was hailed as a hero. The plane he flew on his historic night flight can be seen hanging from the ceiling at Chicago's Museum of Science and Industry.

He worked for United Airlines and established a record of flying 2,400,000 miles in his lifetime, with more than 18,000 hours in the air. In 1937 he retired from flying, wanting a ground job.

Jack had a home in Dune Acres in Porter County, Indiana. In May 1940 the Valparaiso Aero Club invited Captain Jack to give a talk to high school students in Porter County, Indiana, and to be a special guest at a luncheon at Urschel Field's clubhouse.[7]

At the start of World War II, Jack joined the Civil Aeronautics Administration and the Defense Support Corporation to get materials for the war effort. He contracted malaria in the Amazon jungle, where the team was looking for sources of rubber. After a serious fall and weakened by malaria, he was unable to recover. In a fitting tribute to a man who loved to fly, his ashes were scattered over Lake Michigan.

---

7. "Air Ace to Address Local Pupils at High School," *Vidette-Messenger*, May 15, 1940.

The 1938 movie *Men with Wings* was based on his life. Two children's books were also written: *Pilot Jack Knight* by A. M. Anderson and R. E. Johnson and *Jack Knight's Brave Flight* by Jill Esbaum.

Oakley D. (O. D.) Lutes

September 2, 1907–April 30, 1963

Oakley with Stinson 105.

His first name "Oakley" comes from the last name of a female line in his family going back seven to eight generations.[8]

Oakley received his pilot's license around 1926. He was one of the earliest commercial pilots in Porter County, Indiana. In 1928 he was a representative for American Eagle airplanes. He already owned an American Eagle but wanted people to be aware there was a new one coming to the Calumet Air Transport Field at 61st and Broadway in Gary, Indiana. He later sold his American Eagle plane to Carl Harvil.

In September 1929 Oakley flew Chesterton High School Coach Walter Jones to Argos, Indiana. The round trip took 72 minutes. The following month on October 7, 1929, Oakley flew a feature correspondent for *The Vidette-Messenger* over Lake Michigan and northern Porter County.

In May 1939 Oakley broke the altitude record at Urschel Field. Flying his Warner-powered Stinson, he reached an altitude of 15,000 feet.

Oakley wanted to join the Air Force during the war; however, his father and uncle persuaded him not to do so. Around 1941 he moved to Jackson, Michigan, where he purchased a manufacturing plant that subcontracted parts for the Army. After the war he sold real estate. He would fly all around the U.S. for this business.

His son stated that his father died in a crash in 1963 when he was heading home to Michigan from Pennsylvania in a horrible storm. He was flying a Navion, a plane that he loved to fly. The tail of the plane was found miles back from the wreckage. They think the plane might have been struck by lightning.

fly!

Oakley Lutes will fly Sunday from the field opposite Graceland Cemetery on Route 30, weather permitting.

One Passenger . . . $3.00
Two Passengers $2.50 ea.

---

8. Conversation with son Oakley S. on September 13, 2013.

Henry (Happy) DeMass

1907–1984

Henry attended Culver Military Academy from 1923 through 1925.[9] Henry had wanted to learn all he could about aviation, including how to build a plane. In 1923 Culver had just started an aviation program. The program was abandoned after one year.

Henry got into trouble at Culver. The academy had a cannon that was loaded and fired every morning. One time he put stones in the cannon and aimed it at the lake, killing many ducks. Henry's roommate at Culver was the Prince of Siam. The prince wanted Henry to move to Siam and head its air force; Henry declined.

In 1925 after leaving Culver, Henry and his brother Raymond hired John Brown of Kankakee, Illinois, to instruct them in flying. They started a business selling Indian motorcycles in Chesterton. Henry also covered wings of planes. People came from all over for him to work on their planes. Raymond went to work at a Cadillac body shop in Gary and was known for his expertise.

Henry flew all kinds of planes but owned only Jennys. Henry would fly his Jenny whenever he could, often flying it low over the countryside. One day he saw a woman standing in her yard. He waved and she waved back as she had seen him out flying on other days. He landed his plane in her yard, and eventually the two of them married. Her name was Elizabeth Link.

---

9. Phone conversations on August 13, 2013, with son Michael DeMass and on August 14, 2013, with daughter Mary Hale.

DEMASS, RAY & DORA — FARM   Rt. 3
Chesterton   SONS: RAYMOND   160 acres
              and HENRY

Ray Sr. and Dora DeMass were Henry's parents. Often Henry would take his mother up in the plane. She was known to close the shades on the north side of the house so she wouldn't see her sons taking off or landing, as she was scared some-thing would happen to them. Henry did suffer a broken arm from a poor landing close to the house. She made him promise after his first child was born that he would quit flying; he did just that. Mary was born in 1933.

Mary remembers seeing a Jenny in the hangar at the DeMass farm when she was about five years old. She said the plane was very light and that you could almost pick it up with one hand. Mary thinks her father may have built the Jenny from a kit. He sold the Jenny in the late 1930s to Daniel F. Neuman, who won many awards with it. As Daniel was restoring that Jenny, he found the name Henry "Happy" DeMass carved into the end rib wood on one wing. The plane's identification number 2404 was found on the rudder and the wings. This Jenny is now located in Polk City, Florida. It is owned by Kermit Weeks as part of his Fantasy of Flight Museum.

One time Michael went with his father to an air show in Peoria, Illinois. They had a Jenny there. His father looked it over and said, "I would never fly in that death trap." It wasn't put together well; the wires weren't tight, and nothing was up to his specifications. Michael doesn't believe his father ever flew in a commercial plane as a passenger. If he wasn't flying it, he was not going to get into it. Michael said his father

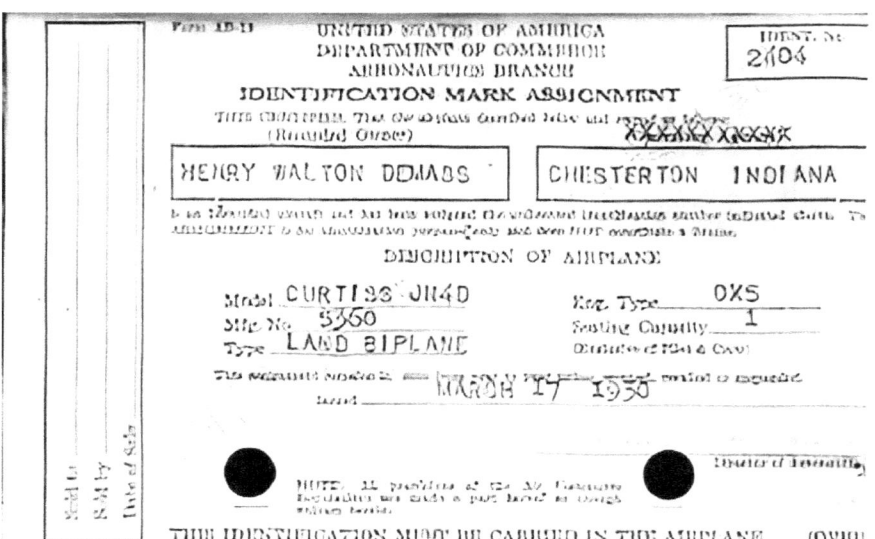

Henry DeMass' official registration card for his 2404 Jenny.

Daniel Neuman finished restoring this Jenny in September 1975 with the help of his son and wife. In 1977 he repainted it a darker olive color.

laughed all the time, so his nickname of "Happy" was apropos. Henry had several jobs in his lifetime. He worked for a Chesterton cemetery vault factory, a well-drilling company, and Inland Steel.

Russell Hankforth

September 9, 1909–April 5, 1959

Russell grew up in Porter, Indiana.[10] Russell was an experienced aviator and mechanic. He owned a flying school and gave exhibition flights. One day Russell took Pearl Linderman up for a ride. After landing and just before they came to a full stop, the engine fell off. In anger he just threw the engine over the fence.

Russell flew Vaughn and Carl Harvil to the races in Indianapolis in May 1928. This trip took two hours in his three-place Laird Swallow.

Russell worked at the airport in Muncie, Indiana. Because he could fly, he was, thankfully, able to be with his mother just before she died in April 1929.

In 1930 Russell had his Laird Swallow biplane on the field in Chesterton. While doing maintenance, a welder had to climb under it with a torch to do repairs. A fire started, resulting in the plane burning to the ground.

Russell did stunts in the 1931 Porter, Indiana, Fourth of July celebration and then went to Hollywood to become an aerial stunt artist. He was a pilot in the 1937 film *Flying High*.

On November 10, 1930, a plane with 17 cases of rum on board was forced down in Columbia, Mississippi. Authorities believed Hankforth was the pilot. In February 1932 Russell and seven other men were indicted on three counts: transportation of intoxicating liquor, receiving and transporting goods that should have been invoiced through the customs department, and conspiracy to violate the National Prohibition Act. Several men went to trial, and the government was dismayed when the charges were dropped due to insufficient evidence. Russell didn't attend any of the trials and could not be found. His friends did not believe Russell was involved in any way.

---

10. Conversations in 2013 with Eva Hopkins, Westchester Township History Museum, Chesterton, Indiana.

Martin (Marty) Rintz
June 29, 1912–January 22, 1962

When Martin was twelve, he was an aviation enthusiast and read everything he could find concerning flying.[11]

He learned about motors at the Harvils' flying field. In 1928 he built his first plane with a motorcycle engine. This plane did not meet specifications, so he took it apart.

In July 1930 Martin at age 17 soloed his 666W monoplane that he had constructed. The cost of the plane, including a water-cooled engine, was $200.

Martin crashed his plane on October 16, 1938, when he took off from a yard and was not able to gain altitude; he hit several sets of wires before crashing. In the plane were passengers Ralph Carmichael Jr. and Leroy Carlson from Crocker, Indiana. They crawled from the demolished plane with only a few bumps and bruises.

MARTY RINTZ PLANE CRASH

11. "Martin Rintz, Looking Backward, 50 Years Ago," *Vidette-Messenger*, July 18, 1980.

Martin was stationed in Europe with his Army Air Forces unit for 18 months during World War II, flying more than 55 missions as a radio gunner during which time he was awarded the Distinguished Flying Cross and Air Medal. Upon his return to civilian life, he operated a television repair shop and was a member of Porter Lodge 2511 Veterans of Foreign Wars.

Carleton Lee (C. Lee) Nelson
November 5, 1890–March 25, 1968

On October 29, 1914, C. Lee was appointed city clerk for Valparaiso, Indiana. He resigned and served in the Army during World War I.[12]

In early 1928 C. Lee was working in Chicago as a city clerk. He grew tired of this work and decided he wanted to fly. In 1928 he attended the Mid-West Airways Corporation School of Flying in Monmouth, Illinois, and then purchased a Taylorcraft from John Livingston at the factory in Alliance, Ohio. Interestingly their paths crossed again in 1941 when John had to make an emergency landing due to a snowstorm at Urschel Field.

C. Lee Nelson received his limited commercial license on August 7, 1929, in Fort Wayne, Indiana. He had his own hangar and plane on a field a mile north and east of the old Valparaiso fairgrounds. The entrance to his field was the road north of Hall's Factory. That same month he advertised in the newspaper flights for $2.50 for two people and $3 for one person. He and Oakley Lutes were two of the first in the vicinity of Valparaiso to own their own planes. In September he was giving fairgoers rides in his plane, and by then he had more than 100 hours in the air. C. Lee flew a passenger from his field to Lafayette, Kokomo, and Fort Wayne, Indiana. They flew a total of 285 miles in 6.5 hours with short stops in each city.

In December 1930 a $20,000 six-place Bellanca monoplane with a 425-horsepower Wasp motor was en route from Newcastle, Delaware, to Minneapolis, Minnesota. It had to make an emergency landing at Nelson's field, as the plane was running low on gas with only 3 gallons in the tank. They were elated to find his field. Elvia Tarkington, a Curtiss-Wright representative, had also made a forced landing at Nelson's field a week earlier.

On December 14, 1934, C. Lee Nelson, Claude Lindberg, and Bud Winder flew their planes over the city of Valparaiso while Bud did several stunts. They were celebrating the 31st Aviation Day, honoring the Wright brothers' historic flight at Kitty Hawk. Bud was keeping his plane at Nelson's field. C. Lee moved his plane to Urschel Field in 1934.

C. Lee Nelson was clerk-treasurer for two administrations starting in 1914 and was the auditor for Porter County in 1948.

---

12. "Nelson Gets Flying Permit," *Vidette-Messenger*, August 8, 1929.

McCool Airport, Portage, Indiana
1929–1948

HARRY DITSLER

McCOOL Ind. CAA STATION c.1933
on Airport Rd. n. of US 6
mail addr. RFD Hobart, Ind.

McCool Airport consisted of a grass airstrip, a beacon, and a small building, which was manned 24 hours a day. McCool was a government emergency airfield for pilots flying from Detroit to Chicago. Originally it was located 8 miles northwest of Valparaiso about a mile north of U.S. Route 6; subsequently, it moved to U.S. Route 6 at 500 West. It was considered one of the better emergency landing fields in Indiana. The beacon at McCool Airport was installed in 1929 by the Bureau of Air Commerce. Henry Ford was instrumental in starting the beacons in this area. Six employees maintained the field and handled the operations.

In 1935 Glen Goddard of Valparaiso actively promoted moving McCool operations to Urschel Field, as he believed McCool was too close to Lake Michigan, where fog often developed. The runways at McCool were only 1,200 feet, whereas Urschel Field runways were 2,500 feet, which could accommodate larger planes.

In April 1936 a Tri-Motor bound for Detroit had to make an emergency landing at McCool due to a snowstorm. Several farmers helped dislodge the plane from the soft ground before it could take off.

In September 1938 McCool Airport placed an ad in the paper offering rides on a giant 14-passenger Tri-Motor airplane. The cost was 50 cents during the day, increasing to $1 for night rides. Hamer Flying Service was providing this service.

Ford Tri-Motor at McCool in 1935

Charles Lucas, a member of the Valparaiso Aero Club, had to solo at McCool Field since Urschel Field was in no condition for new students to take off or land without great peril.

McCool closed on March 1, 1948, when the U.S. government gave up the lease with Ross Crisman for his 51 acres used as the airport. They believed emergency airfields were no longer needed, even though over the years, many pilots had used this field for an emergency landing when they had trouble with their motors or were running low on fuel. Crisman could not find any other prospects for keeping an airfield and decided it would be more profitable to return the land to farming.

The half acre where the beacon was located would still be maintained by the CAA. The beacon and markers were moved to Porter County Airport in 1955.

Henry Foster

June 7, 1910–December 25, 1984

Henry took his first flying lesson in 1930 at Bud Winder's field south of U.S. Route 30, which was four years before he flew at Urschel Field.[13] He first soloed in a glider towed behind a car with a 500-foot rope.

Bud Winder, Bun Blackman, Axel Nogard Jr., Bob Ulsh, Henry Foster

In July 1936 Henry increased his solo hours in the Waco training plane that the club had recently purchased; Bud Winder was his instructor. Many members of the original Aero Club also practiced in that Waco. In December 1936 Henry received his pilot's license at the Gary Airport. He received his air transport license in 1937. Henry described flying:

> There was a thrill there. It was something everybody looked up to. You wore a helmet and goggles; I even had boots and knicker-laced pants like Roscoe Turner. There was something you were doing that everybody didn't do.[14]

13. "Airport News," *Vidette-Messenger*, December 26, 1936.
14. Robert Foster and Ruth Sevier Foster, "Henry Starr Foster: National Air and Space Museum," Henry Starr Foster | National Air and Space Museum, accessed June 22, 2023, https://airandspace.si.edu/support/wall-of-honor/henry-starr-foster.

In October 1938 Henry piloted a plane over the Valparaiso University homecoming football game. Bud Winder dropped a streamer-decorated football out of the plane, and the ball hit the 40-yard line.

With more than 500 hours of flying time, Henry appeared in the big August 1939 air show at Urschel Field. The spectators saw pilots do low-to-the-ground crazy flying stunts. Those included ribbon cutting, car bombing, handkerchief pickup, and parachute jumping. Other local pilots were Bud Winder, Axel Nogard Jr., and Rollie Humphrey.[15] Henry was one of the charter members of the first Valparaiso Aero Club and had appeared in air shows in Indiana and Illinois. By then he had earned his commercial license. He believed flying was an expensive pastime and getting hours in a plane was a tough proposition.

Henry picked up Urschel Field's new J-3 Cub 60 trainer plane in Lock Haven, Pennsylvania, in May 1940. Three months later on August 15, he passed his final instructor flight test at Sky Harbor Airport in Northbrook, Illinois. He then became an instructor at the Winder Flying School at Urschel Field.

In 1941 he left for Pine Bluff, Arkansas, to be an instructor at the Aeronautical Flying Cadet School, which was a unit of the U.S. Army Air Corps training program. Before he left, he had been the manager of Urschel Field. In August 1944 Henry left for duties as a Civil Aeronautics Administration (CAA) inspector for North and South Carolina. For 30 years Henry was in the CAA/FAA in many different administrative capacities in seven states.

After his illustrious career, he retired in 1972 and is fittingly commemorated on the Wall of Honor at the National Air and Space Museum.

---

15. "Henry Foster to Thrill Folks at Valpo Aero Show," *Vidette-Messenger*, August 19, 1939.

Lawrence Marquis (Mark) Murvihill

November 3, 1909–January 4, 1994

Mark's family lived on Campbell Street in Valparaiso, Indiana, when he was very young.[16] Mark learned to fly at Urschel Field sometime in the 1930s. Mark was color blind; to pass tests in the service, he had to spend months training his brain to see the differences between red and green. In the U.S. Army, Mark was learning to be a glider pilot in The Army Glider Service. Since the gliders were not very efficient, the program was curtailed. Mark then became a liaison pilot fighting in the European Theater during World War II. He flew an unarmed plane delivering mail, among other things. He also flew General Matthew Ridgway on many occasions. One time the plane was having trouble, and they had to find a place to land. They were told that the only field available might be loaded with land mines, and if they successfully landed, they were not to get out of the plane. People would be sent to safely come and get them. The general was impatient; he got out of the plane, stepped on a mine, lived through it, and was awarded a Purple Heart. Mark was one of the first to go into a concentration camp after its liberation. His family had some of the pictures that he took. Understandably, he never spoke of the war. Afterward in 1946 he went to Colorado for a year, working as a pilot for the U.S. Fish and Wildlife Service.

Mark had his A&E mechanic license. He attended the Lewis School of Aeronautics using the GI Bill. Mark signed a business lease in early 1948 with William Urschel for the use of a green-painted wood building northeast of the hangars. That building had been part of the Civilian Conservation Corps (CCC) Camp. When Mark was at Urschel Field, he repaired engines and replaced cloth coverings on the airplanes. Mark would test the tensile strength of the fabric on the planes. The plane's fabric was sewn by hand. Then seven to nine layers of dope (a varnish

16. Conversations with Mark's niece Margaret and her husband Larry Eggleston on February 1, 2013, and July 3, 2023.

applied to the fabric surface of aircraft to strengthen them and keep them airtight) were applied to the fabric. Sometimes he hired high school boys to help him.

Much of the information about Mark came from interviewing Mark's niece Margaret, who had lived with Mark and his parents. When she was young, Margaret spent most summer days around Mark's business at Urschel Field, accompanied by her dog. She wanted to play the pinball machine in the office, but Mark told her that was off-limits, as it was for the pilots. She spent many hours walking around the top of the walls of the crumbling leftover CCC buildings.

Margaret recalled that across from the CCC camp on the east side of Calumet Avenue was a very large white house with two entrances, used to house the camp's top officers. After the camp left, the Chamber family lived in that house.

Mark took Margaret up for her first ride when she was five years old, flying over all the lakes. She will never forget that day. She thought that each lake looked like a mirror in an artificial setting. Mark also gave a ride to Larry Eggleston when he was about six years old. He loved flying over the lakes and thought the water looked very clean. Some of these lakes were Flint, Wauhob, and Long. He has never forgotten that thrilling day.

Margaret remembered Olie Sundelin as he often visited Mark and made such strong coffee that Mark would comment how a spoon could stand up in that coffee; it was that strong.

Margaret also recalled the Interurban rail line, which ran until October 23, 1938. That rail line was losing ridership as people started buying automobiles. The Interurban was also called "Airline," since the wires were up in the air. One route was on the west side of Calumet Avenue, so it was easy for people to come to Urschel Field.

When Mark moved his business to Porter County Airport, he was the first business on the new road at the airport. This road is now named after him. He expanded his business to include many other services. He maintained planes, performed inspections, trained pilots, ran a charter service, rented aircraft, and instructed mechanics.

MARK MURVIHILL   In doorway of business at Urschel Field

Raymond DeMass

March 20, 1909–October 29, 1971

Raymond DeMass 1929

Raymond learned to fly when he was about twelve years old and owned 13 different kinds of aircraft in his lifetime.[17]

A leg injury from a motorcycle accident in the 1930s prevented him from serving in the armed forces during World War II. Ray was basically a farmer but did work at a Cadillac body shop in Gary, Indiana. Chestnut Hill subdivision in Chesterton, Indiana, is built on the property of their old farm.

Raymond sat his young son David on his lap in an open cockpit plane, and they would go upside down over the cornfields. Maybe this was the reason David never secured his pilot's license. Raymond always had a roll of Tums with him. One time he took someone for a ride, and the man had

PILOT'S DAILY LOG

DATE	FROM	TO	Time In Air	Miles Flown	Total Enl. Hrs.	Weather	Mot. Kt.	DETAIL OF FLIGHT
Brought Forward	1986-30	1930			641'-0%"			*Raymond DeMass*
3-23-31		1931			3 30			
3-24-31	Local (Chesterton)				5 15			*Raymond DeMass*
3-25-31	"	"			4 15			
					65% 0%			

State of Indiana
County of Porter ss

This is to certify that the above statement is correct and True

Subscribed and sworn to before me
this 25th day of march 1931

Carried Forward   arthur rzick, notary Public

WAX FREE   ·TP· AERO MOTOR LUBRICATING OIL   PARAFFIN BASE

---

17. Conversations on June 11, 2013, with daughter Sharon DeMass Lee and on June 18, 2013, with son David.

eaten the whole roll of Tums while they were in the air. Apparently, that man was extremely scared.

Raymond's daughter Sharon recalled flying with her dad when she was three years old in a Vultee, a two-seater Army trainer plane purchased from a Navy training base in about 1942. He kept the plane for about five years. Her father would fly upside down really low over the houses, terrifying and scaring the neighbors. She thinks he kept the plane at the Michigan City Airport, although he may have kept it at Joe Phillips' Airport. This was the last plane he owned.

She also remembers, as a little girl, seeing in a shed just the shell of the Jenny owned by her dad and Uncle Henry. Sharon knew the Harvil twins and the fact that George and Fred drove school buses for a while; however, off duty they would drive their stock cars fast on Fifth Street in Chesterton. To make a point, their cousin once blocked the road with a tractor and a hay wagon to curtail their recklessness.

Probably the most interesting story about Ray centers on how he helped a lady who flew in and landed at Urschel Field. She was afraid to take off since she felt the runway was too short. Raymond said he would fly it out; he made it over the fence and flew it to the Gary Airport, where she retrieved it. Raymond was sworn to secrecy as to the identity of the woman. Rumor has it that the lady was Amelia Earhart.

Form AB-19

DEPARTMENT OF COMMERCE
AERONAUTICS BRANCH

Application No.

APPLICATION FOR PILOT'S LICENSE

License No.

To the Secretary of Commerce:

Application is hereby made for a ___TRANSPORT___ PILOT'S LICENSE.
(Transport, limited commercial, industrial, private, or student)

1. Name __RAYMOND DEMASS__
(Print or type)

2. Permanent address __Chesterton__
(Street) (Post office)
__INDIANA__ __PORTER__ __512W3__
(State) (County) (Telephone)
NOTE—Applicant must advise of any change of address.

3. Place of birth __CHESTERTON, INDIANA__

4. Date of birth __MARCH 20, 1909__ Age last birthday __20__

5. Description of applicant:
Weight __150__ Height __5'11½"__ Color hair d. __BROWN__ Color eyes __blue__

6. Citizenship __AMERICAN__ Race __White__
If alien, what country? ___ (White) (Negro)

7. If alien, and only declaration of intention to become a citizen of the
United States has been filed, state the following:
(a) Serial number of declaration ___ Date of filing ___
(b) State, city, and court in which filed ___

8. Have you previously applied for any class of pilot's license? __YES__
If so, list the following information:
(a) Class of license __PRIVATE__
(b) Were you approved or disapproved? __Approved__
(c) Date examined ___ or within few days of that date __1928__
(d) Place of examination __CHESTERTON, INDIANA__
NOTE—If examined more than once, answer for last examination only.

9. Do you now hold any class of Pilot's License issued by the Department of Commerce? __No__
If so, state class and number? ___

10. Have you ever held a Student Pilot's Permit? __No__ If so, state number ___

11. If application is for a Limited Commercial Pilot's License, name:
(a) Airport or field from which you will operate as base ___
(b) Address of base ___

12. If application is for a Student Pilot's Permit, name:
(a) School ___ Address ___
(b) Airport or field ___ Address ___
(c) Name of instructor ___

13. Date of last physical examination __Aug. 15, 1929__

14. Resident during past five years __Chesterton, Indiana — 3mo at__
__El Dorado, Arkansas__

15. Place most convenient for applicant to take the required pilot's examinations and flight test:
(a) Airport or field __Chesterton Airfield__
(b) Address __" Indiana__

16. Address to which Department of Commerce inspector can MAIL, TELEGRAPH, or TELEPHONE
applicant notice of time and place of examinations:

__Chesterton__
(Street) (Post office)
__INDIANA__ __PORTER__ __512W3__
(State) (County) (Telephone)

NOTE—Failure to respond to such notice is grounds for cancellation of application and letter of authority.

Application must be submitted to the Secretary of Commerce, Washington, D. C., in duplicate, the original of which
must be notarized, accompanied by two identical photographs, showing head and shoulders only, 1½ x 1½ inches
in size. Unless all questions are answered, it will be necessary to return the application.
A fee is not required. In event applicant's address is changed, this office should be notified immediately.

11—4774

APPROVED

DISAPPROVED

Recommended for

Name base if for limited
commercial

Date

Inspector

30

17. Education, including air courses: _High School, flying courses and [illegible], and Engineering, Automatic Instruction work and through [illegible] aviation and special schools_

18. Experience as pilot:
   (a) Name flying fields where you received instruction and their locations: _Was taught to fly at [illegible], Roselawn, and [illegible] field used for flying field_
   (b) Name instructors and give dates: _John Bryant from Momence, Illinois. [illegible] 1925_
   (c) Solo hours in last 90 days _212_ Name fields and give dates _Of Sandy, Wisconsin, private field; Cross country from town to Southern Stations, Illinois, through Kansas City, Mo., to Chehalis, Indiana_
   (d) Solo hours in last year _380_ Name fields and give dates, omitting those listed above _Chesterton, Indiana, local field; Battle Rock, Wis.; Fairfax ind.; Kansas City; Calumet, Michigan_
   (e) Total solo hours _650_ Name fields and give dates, omitting those listed above _[several lines illegible] Indiana, mostly, [illegible], [illegible], Illinois, Missouri, Iowa, Kansas, Nebraska, Louisiana, Texas, Mississippi, Dakota from [illegible]_
   (f) Name types flown and hours in each _Jenner 250; Jenny 125; Standard 25; Travel Air 10; Eaglerock 15; American Eagle 250_
   (g) Night flying experience _23 hours, cross country + local flights_

19. Experience and training on aircraft engines, giving types with which familiar and length of experience in each _OX5 [illegible]; Hisso 300; [illegible] + [illegible]; OXX6 - 4 y.; LeRhone [illegible]; Packard; LeBlond; Wrights + Curtiss_

20. Experience as to airplane structure and rigging, giving types with which familiar and length of experience in each _[illegible]; Jenny; Standard - 4 y.; [illegible]; [illegible]; [illegible]; Eaglerock - 1 y.; American Eagle 2 y._

21. Have you read the Air Commerce Regulations? _Yes_

22. AFFIDAVIT:
   State _Indiana_
   County _Porter_

I hereby swear that the statements contained in this application are true.

Dated this _7_ day of _October_, 1928

Subscribed and sworn to before me this _7_ day of _October_, 1928

My commission expires _[illegible]_, 1932.

DIRECTIONS

1. Application for only one class of license should be made.
2. The physical examination must be taken before an authorized medical examiner of the Department of Commerce. In case you are a regular or reserve pilot of the Army, Navy, or Marine Corps, you may instead submit a certified copy of an Army or Navy physical examination for flying, if such examination has been made within the last six months. Certificate of the result of such examination will not be accepted, but an actual copy of the examiner's report is required, which he will forward direct to this Department upon request from you to do so. No action will be taken on this application until the report of physical examination has been received.
3. The applicant will be notified of the time and place of the holding of the required examinations and tests. He must furnish the airplane for the tests involved.
4. In answering question 18 give only your experience as pilot; that is, as the sole operator of the controls and in command of aircraft in flight.

31

Erick (Olie) Sundelin

August 7, 1910–November 30, 1979

Another early Porter County aviator was Swedish-born Olie. On September 26, 1938, Olie and his wife Lucille were flying when the propeller of their small aircraft cracked at 2,000 feet. The plane shook violently as Olie landed in a small field about 5 miles east of Westville, Indiana. They weren't hurt.

Just about a month later on October 30, 1938, Olie and Bun Blackman crashed in a cornfield east of Boone Grove on Bert Thatcher's farm about 7 miles from Valparaiso. They were severely injured and spent many weeks in the hospital. Olie suffered compound fractures in both legs, and Bun fractured his right arm and leg.

October 30, 1938 crash.

Olie Sundelin, Arthur Babcock, and Maury Anderson began building a plane in Olie's basement in 1948.[18] Two years later the Knight Twister had its inaugural flight. The guys continued to do test flights at Urschel

---

18. "Three Valparaiso Men Build Tiny 15-Foot Plane," *Vidette-Messanger*, November 2, 1951.

Field to tweak updates, such as increasing the length of the nose and the plane's speed to 160 miles an hour. How fitting that this plane currently hangs from the ceiling of the large conference room at Urschel Laboratories, Inc., where Olie worked for 47 years.

Three Valparaiso Men Build Tiny 15-Foot Plane

WEATHER PERMITTING, Valparaiso area residents will see this small plane being put through continued test flights the next several weekends. The plane, built by Olaf Sundelin, Arthur Babcock and Maurice Anderson, has a 14-foot wing-span and 15-foot fuselage and weighs 800 pounds. Top speed of the "Knight Twister" is about 160 miles an hour. The plane's design lends itself well to acrobatics. It is believed to be one of the smallest aircraft in the midwest.   (Photo by Marshall Weinstein)

Olie was very involved with the Civil Air Patrol (CAP). In 1952 Olie and Ted Falls flew to Waco, Texas, to pick up an L-18 plane at Waco's Connally Air Force Base. The plane was used to take the members of the CAP up for orientation flights. They hoped these flights would get CAP teenagers interested and engaged in flying. The cadets were fifteen to eighteen years old. Olie was an instructor and participated in the air shows at Urschel Field. He was also a member of the Coast Guard Reserve.

Irvine (Vance) Ulsh

January 2, 1890–September 29, 1944

Charles Bernard Ulsh	Robert Vance Ulsh	Helen Mae Ulsh Eaton
2/13/1915–2/29/1966	*1917–11/24/1999*	*1/30/1920–5/1/2008*

Vance and three of his children were very involved in flying at Urschel Field. In 1928 Robert, 11, and Bernard, 13, flew in a motorized OX Waco NC54798 flown by C. Lee Nelson. The boys were hooked. Robert soloed in the same plane in May 1939 under the watchful eye of his instructors, Axel Nogard Jr. and Bud Winder.

Bernard and Robert were early members of the first Valparaiso Aero Club. Their sister Helen Mae soloed on September 11, 1941, becoming the third family member to be flying.

She was also the third female to have soloed at Urschel Field. Preceding her was Nena Winder Babcock, followed by Bette Nogard. When Helen Mae soloed, her father decided he would begin flying lessons, becoming the fourth in his family to fly.

Vance encouraged his sons to get their instructor's rating, which they did. Among the pilots who flew out of Urschel Field, Vance was known to be always cheerful, never having a bad word to say about anyone. Always encouraging, they considered him to be a pilot's true friend. He is remembered for always telling pilots not to stretch a glide.

In June 1937, 48 planes participated in the Ninth Annual Indiana Air Tour, taking them from Gary to Michigan City, Rensselaer, Rochester, Fort Wayne, Kokomo, and Muncie. After they left Gary, dense fog caused the flying ceiling to drop almost to zero. All planes landed safely without any damage or injury to the pilots. Most landed on the beach near Lake Michigan, some in any field they could find, while Bernard Ulsh and Axel Nogard Jr., flying a Waco plane, landed at Urschel Field.

Both brothers worked at Urschel Field. Bernard was an airplane mechanic while he continued to barnstorm in northern Indiana with his mentor, Axel Nogard. Robert was an instructor with Wings Field, Inc. in the federal Civilian Pilot Training Program (CPTP), which was signed into law on June 27, 1939. The program's purpose was to increase the number of knowledgeable pilots for possible military use.

In 1942 Bernard was a squadron leader in the Civil Air Patrol (CAP). The slogan for the club during the war was, "Join the CAPs and whip the Japs."

In March 1943 Robert was appointed supervisor in charge of students for the U.S. Army Air Forces at LaGuardia Field in New York City. He was the fifth person from the Valparaiso Aero Club to join the Civil Aeronautics Administration (CAA). The others were Bud Winder, Axel Nogard Jr., Henry Foster, and Rollie Humphrey. During World War II he was also a production test pilot for the Grumman Avenger torpedo bomber. After the war he worked 36 years for Chevron, retiring in 1982 having logged 20,000 hours in the air.

Glen Goddard

April 19, 1889–February 17, 1946

In 1914 Glen came to Porter County to farm and four years later settled in Valparaiso as he pursued his real estate interests. On September 17, 1931, Glen soloed and flew to Crown Point, Indiana. Five years before he started flying, he began his unofficial role as Porter County's aviation booster. His foresight and energy did much to enhance aviation in the Valparaiso area.

Glen and William Urschel shared that same vision, and together they worked from many different angles to promote aviation during its infancy for the greater good of Porter County. On December 22, 1933, Glen and William submitted to the Valparaiso City Council documents showing the federal government was willing to grant money to help improve airports.[19] This money was available only to public airports, not privately held ones, as Urschel Field was at that time. The city needed to buy or lease the land, and these two men facilitated that requirement by presenting the city with a more-than-fair contract for leasing Urschel Field.

In March 1934 Glen worked diligently with Fred Hoke, the chairman of the Indiana Civil Works Administration (CWA) in Indianapolis, and Major Charles E. Cox Jr., the airport advisor for the CWA, to secure government funds to grade Urschel Field. These funds were obtained, and work started on the airport in May 1934. Bud Winder shortly thereafter moved his hangar and planes to Urschel Field, as he became the airport manager.

Involved in many facets of aviation, Glen responded to concerns in February 1935 that he was going to take parties up to fly over the nudist colony in Valparaiso. He stated, "I fly so high two fairies in the altogether gliding through the shady umbrage would look just about like two polka dots on a guinea hen."[20]

In April 1935 Glen purchased a Stinson four-passenger plane with electric lights, an electric starter, and brakes. This Stinson could fly up to 125 miles an hour. Bud Winder would be doing the flying, as he was more experienced. Glen kept that plane at the Chicago-Hammond Airport in

---

19. "Glen J. Goddard Proposes Airport Project Under CWA," *Vidette-Messenger*, December 23, 1933.
20. "Goddard Buys Plane; Will Park It Here," *Vidette-Messenger*, April 19, 1935.

Lansing, Illinois, but planned on bringing it to Urschel Field when the long-sought-after airport hangar was finished.

In July 1936 it was Glen who tried to persuade the federal government to transfer all the activities from McCool Airport to Urschel Field. Urschel Field was better suited as an emergency field for the government because it had fewer storms, less fog, and lower wind velocity. The government's 20-year lease ended on March 1, 1948. Ross Crisman, who owned the McCool land, decided to farm the 57 acres after the airport's closure when his efforts at keeping it open failed. McCool's beacon and lights remained at McCool for a while after its closure, but eventually, the beacon was moved to Porter County Airport.

Ever the flying enthusiast, Glen knew that his friend Paul E. Marks had a great aversion to flying. Knowing this, on August 10, 1935, Glen invited Paul to get in to look at his Stinson's instrument panel. Someone at the airport slammed the door shut, and off they went. After landing Paul declared, "I'm ready for another airplane ride. Gee, it's keen."[21]

Another avenue in cultivating public interest in flying was the presentation of an air circus. In June 1935 Glen, Bud Winder, and William Younce went to Rensselaer, Indiana, to present an air circus, where they would entertain the public with aerial stunts. They had planned to do this type of program at Urschel Field when it was completed.

As a multifaceted businessman, Glen was also an agent for American Air Lines. In the May 11, 1936, *Vidette-Messenger*, he placed an ad for a flight on the Hindenburg airship to the summer German Olympic games. The fare was $400 one way or $720 round trip. During the summer of 1936, ten round trips from New Jersey to Liverpool were successfully completed. Misfortune struck the following spring when on May 6, 1937, the infamous Hindenburg airship crashed and killed 36 people out of the 97 who were on board.

No history of early aviation in Porter County would be complete without an article recognizing Glen's part in the advancement of aviation during the industry's infancy. His dedication and countless efforts to ensure the optimal environment to utilize the talents of his aviation colleagues have surely earned him our gratitude.

---

21. "Kidnapping," *Vidette-Messenger*, August 10, 1935.

Claude Lindberg
May 3, 1905–June 9, 1963

Claude was a contractor and built many homes in Porter County, as well as being the manager at Urschel Field from 1943 until 1948 and the airport's chief instructor.

Under Claude's guidance, several improvements had been made at Urschel Field, such as lengthening the runways to 2,680 feet. Claude was also in charge of providing markers to help pilots identify cities and towns. They planned to put markers on the roofs of the hangars.

One interesting incident involving Claude happened on September 11, 1945, when the watchdog's barking awakened him around 3 a.m. He found the north door of the hangar open and that a plane was missing. Two Chesterton High School students flew in the dark for 50 miles before landing at South Bend Airport. Ronnie Smalley, 15, and Richard Fenters, 14, flew a Cub that belonged to the Chesterton Aero Club after hiding in a locked hangar at Urschel Field. When their gas was running low, they saw the lights of South Bend Airport and landed. They were called to the tower for questioning since they did not have navigation lights. The inspector at the airport stated that the gas was nearly depleted, and he was surprised they didn't kill themselves. Neither one had a pilot's license. They hitchhiked home.

In July 1945 Claude was president of the 15-member Urschel Field Aero Club. The Aero Club had trained more than 900 pilots since the airport had opened, and many of those were flying all over the world in the service to their country.

Claude had been certified as an official assistant CAA inspector. He also had a class of 20 air students at Medaryville in Pulaski County, Indiana, in February 1945. They flew from a field northeast of town.

Medaryville was typical of many embryo airports all over the United States.[22]

Claude had more than 8,000 hours of flying time by February 1956. At that time his 17-year-old daughter Judy soloed after 45 minutes of instruction in a dual-controlled plane. She was in the air for 15 minutes. She had taken off on a snow-packed runway on skis. Judy stated that her father never bawled her out over some minor infraction, but the motors made so much noise she probably would not have heard him anyway. Her mother said she hoped to be Judy's first passenger after she got her license.

At the time of Claude's death in 1963, he was giving flight instructions at the Porter County Airport. An aviator to the end!

22. "Local Airport as Feeder Line Stop Being Sought," *Vidette-Messenger*, July 20, 1945.

Axel Nogard Jr.
April 26, 1912–September 27, 2000

Axel was in the first Aero Club at Urschel Field in 1936. Earlier he had been in the Aero Club at Bud Winder's field.[23]

In 1936 he took one of his solo flights to Lafayette, Indiana, stating that travel by plane beats an automobile, as that flight took him only 45 minutes. He stated that Urschel Field was in deplorable condition when the city no longer wanted to lease it. Many deep holes in the field, tall weeds, and deep ditches made using the field dangerous. McCool Airport was a better option. Axel received his commercial license in December 1938 and his instructor's license five months later in South Bend, Indiana.

On October 11, 1936, the Aero Club put on an air show called the Amateur Air Show. In July 1938 Axel and 20 other pilots were on the Air Tour, sponsored by the Northern Indiana Pilots' Council. Pilots came from all the stops on the tour: Gary, LaPorte, Michigan City, New Chicago, Hobart, and Valparaiso.

---

23. "Airport Notes," *Vidette-Messenger*, October 3, 1936.

The following year Axel and Bernard Ulsh left for Terre Haute, Indiana, in Axel's Waco plane with an OX-5 motor. They were joining the Indiana Air Tour, sponsored by the Indiana Aircraft Association and the Indiana Pilots' Association. Thousands gathered to watch all the flying antics. Axel was a prominent pilot in that air show.

Axel and Bud Winder were honored for being the first instructors in the state to have all their students receive their private pilot's license. CAA inspector George Murchison came to Urschel Field in 1941 to see the last two students who had taken the government course at Valparaiso University and Winder Flying School at Urschel Field. The inspector praised the university, the flying school, and the students for completing this course in such a rapid fashion.

Axel was one of four pilots who flew to Florida for the January 1941 Miami Air Races. They flew a total of 3,500 miles on that trip. The other pilots were Robert Ulsh, Arthur Babcock, and Lawrence Gesse.

Axel left Valparaiso in April 1941 to work as a Civil Aeronautics Administration (CAA) inspector at LaGuardia Field in New York.

After that Axel was transferred to West Virginia, Pennsylvania, New Jersey, and Maryland. In 1951 while employed as a supervising agent of the Baltimore Aviation District Office of the CAA, he was awarded the Pfeiffer Award for his outstanding work in the advancement of private flying.

In August 1945 a DC-3 landed at Urschel Field to board Axel, his three sisters, and other friends for a flight to Lake George, New York. Remarkably, that plane, piloted by Ed Rogers and Randy Mehlerin, easily took off with 13 people onboard.

Lawrence Gesse
June 9, 1917–September 8, 1974

Five Gesse brothers were in World War II, but it was Lawrence who flew a lot of planes while in the Navy. Lawrence learned to fly from Bud Winder, Olie Sundelin, and Henry Foster.[24] In later years Lawrence lived in Charlotte, North Carolina, and flew for a man who owned a chain of restaurants called S & W Cafeterias. He flew a twin-engine B-17 for this gentleman. Lawrence died of a heart attack at age 57.

Lawrence Gesse, Norman Danielson, ? Schroeder, George Rickard, Betty Mogard Richards

William often flew with his brother Lawrence, especially to their farm in Kouts, Indiana, and then back to Valparaiso. He stated that the big threshers' dinner at the end of the season made threshing somewhat more bearable. Threshing always seemed to be done in the hottest weather, and it was really dirty, hard work. Different farm families would get together and help each other get the work done. The women cooked for days, making huge amounts of food. Especially memorable were the many kinds of pies. He stated that the women wanted the men to eat all

24. Conversation with brother William Gesse in 2013.

the food and kept filling up their plates. One time Olie, Henry, and Bud flew down for this big yearly dinner. They felt sick from all the food they felt they had to eat and uneasily took off for home in Valparaiso with very full stomachs.

One day William had a chocolate malt somewhere in downtown Valparaiso. His brother Lawrence was headed to their farm in Kouts, so William, having finished his malt, decided to fly with him. Just so happens that William had a very nice hat on that day. He started feeling sick and took his hat off and "filled it." He told his brother he didn't want to get the airplane messed up. As they flew over the city, Lawrence grabbed the hat and flung it out of the Cub. William hoped the contents did not hit anyone in downtown Valparaiso.

In January 1941 Lawrence flew with several pilots from Urschel Field to an air show in Miami, Florida. He had never flown that far from home and felt very uneasy flying over the large marshes and other areas that could be unsafe for landing. Around Valparaiso one could land in just about any field.

Lawrence's brother Floyd Gesse also flew. In a phone conversation

with Floyd's son Brian on August 27, 2013, he recalled that dad Floyd was a farmer by trade who had learned to fly at Urschel Field. Rumor had it that Floyd did not possess any innate flying acumen and probably should not have been flying. Brian's parents were married in 1942, and Floyd quit flying after having several children. His wife told him she was down on the ground taking care of the babies, and he was up in the air flying. Floyd died of a heart attack at the age of 64.

Floyd Gesse

Ralph Barneko
May 22, 1912–March 4, 1977

Around 1930 Ralph and his cousin built a plane, and his cousin was the first to fly it. He crashed it into the soft marsh near Wolf's Corners. Ralph then started to build another plane.

In 1931 at Bud Winder's airfield, the newly christened Aero Club had 14 members. Ralph was one of them.[25] A glider kit to be used for instruction had been purchased; club members were assembling it.

Ralph and A. W. Shinabarger, a mechanic of 34 years, worked on an old Curtiss Army plane in A. W.'s garage on Campbell Street in Valparaiso. They wanted to use their plane for advertising purposes and planned on doing a test flight at Barneko Field, which was 1/4 mile east of Wolf's Corners. The

Lindberg, Winder, and Barneko July, 1936

field was 90 by 30 rods. A. W. rebuilt the engine while Ralph worked on the plane. Sadly, a neighbor boy climbed a tree to watch what Ralph was doing and was electrocuted on some wires. When the plane was completed, Bud Winder flew it about ten times.

In 1936 Ralph received his pilot's license and an aviation mechanic's license. Three years later Ralph passed his written and flight test for a commercial license in South Bend, Indiana.

In August 1939 at Urschel Field, Ralph was welding the tail of an aircraft owned by someone in Kouts, Indiana, when it caught on fire. He succeeded in pushing it out of the hangar; however, he received burns on his face and hands. Everyone believed they were very fortunate since the hangar full of planes did not burn down.[26]

At a meeting of the Valparaiso Aero Club, Ralph became a member of what they called the "He Pulled a Boner" club. Ralph had made a

25. "Anxious for an Airport," *Vidette-Messenger*, August 30, 1932.
26. "Fire Destroys a Plane," *Vidette-Messenger*, August 21, 1939.

flight over Valparaiso thinking a passenger was in the back of the plane. After landing he realized the passenger had never jumped into the plane.

During World War II Ralph was a flying instructor for Army cadets at the Helena Technical School in Helena, Arkansas, reaching the rank of a lieutenant commander in the U.S. Navy.

Nena Winder Babcock

October 15, 1921–November 10, 2013

John (Bud) Winder

October 22, 1912–May 4, 1989

Nena was born in Springerton, Illinois.[27] Her family moved to Mt. Vernon, Illinois, where her father and brother Bud worked at a boxcar factory. The company closed, so they came to live in Valparaiso, where they worked at a boxcar company at Indiana Harbor. Nena claimed the nine-year age gap between her and Bud resulted in them not being as close as many siblings.

Many members of their family lived in an apartment building near Valparaiso University. Bud met and married Mabel Sheets. Mabel mentioned to Bud that maybe aviation would be a good business to get into. Bud had learned to fly as a teenager. He took a ground course in Chicago at age sixteen and a year later went to South Bend, Indiana, to learn to fly, as there were no instructors in the vicinity. His instructor was Homer Stockert of the Stockert Flying Service. Mabel worked at the telephone company to earn money to pay the costs of Bud's pilot's license.

---

27. Conversation on August 29, 2012.

In 1930 Bud built an airfield south of U.S. Route 30 across from what is now Porter County Airport on land he leased from the Evans family. Bud's first plane was a double-winged Waco. Soon after he bought a glider and then a Piper Cub, which he used to give lessons. The field he used was 15 acres and was shared with horses and cows.

FLY!

With Bud Winder

Licensed Plane Pilot

also

Glider Flying

Airport 2 Miles East on

U. S. 30

Nena remembers her family often clearing away the rocks, so Bud would not wreck his plane when landing. On one occasion in November 1931, Bud took "Broncho" John Sullivan up for a ride from C. Lee Nelson's field. John was one of the few remaining Indian scouts and had served in many wars. He was induced to make the ride while suffering a terrible headache. On landing his headache was gone!

In September 1932 Bud received his air transport license from the

U.S. Department of Commerce. Bud organized a glider aero club with 14 members in March 1933 at his field.

The first time Bud took people up in a plane, he would do loops and scare them. Bud had a funny sense of humor, as evidenced by the time he electrified a porch swing and would laugh when people sat in it. Bud and many of his friends would put on air shows all over the state to earn money. Nena said they did some crazy stunts in those days, such as flying low to pick up a piece of material attached to a stick on the ground.

Bud and his friend William Urschel were instrumental in getting aviation started in Valparaiso. On May 18, 1934, Bud moved his hangar, a glider, and a Waco open-cockpit two-place plane from Evans' farm to Urschel Field, where he would manage the field. In the back of the hangar was a small apartment for Bud, his wife, and new baby Dixie Lee, delivered by Dr. Van Winkle. Later the Winders would live in an apartment on Jefferson Street and then at the farmhouse at Urschel Field.

In 1934 the Valparaiso Aero Club was formed, initially to help those interested in aviation to buy a plane together, making flight time less expensive.

In January 1936 Bud was offered the manager's job at LaPorte Airport. The offer was appealing if Valparaiso didn't get the money to complete Urschel Field, but he did not find it necessary to leave Urschel Field. Later in August of that same year, Bud planned an air show to celebrate the Porter County Centennial at Urschel Field, where attendance was upward of 2,000 spectators.

As an airport jack-of-all-trades, Bud even was called to formally witness the wedding of Lenora Middleton and Fred Salter in October 1936. The couple had landed at Urschel Field in a chartered plane, expressing a desire to get married. Fred, originally from Chicago and then Los Angeles, was in real estate, and Lenora was a Hollywood actress for Warner Bros.

Bud and Olie Sundelin in 1937

In February 1937 Bud took over as manager of Urschel Field after the city canceled their lease. He produced many air shows to raise money to improve the field and taught hundreds of people to become pilots without one mishap. In May 1938 Bud advertised that one could learn to fly in a Taylor Cub for approximately $40 at his Winder Flying Service.

On June 9, 1939, Nena was visiting Bud's family one afternoon when what was described as a tornado hit the airport. The hangar and Bud's two planes were destroyed. Nena, Mabel, and Dixie Lee were buried under the debris; fortunately, all survived. Nena saw her brother standing in the rain, looking at the utter devastation of the hangar, planes, and business with tears streaming down his face. It was just heartbreaking for him. With the help of William Urschel, Valparaiso Aero Club members, and many others, a bigger and better hangar was built. Bud persisted, and before long the business was again viable. William Urschel built an airport office, a little house, and eventually the north hangar. He built the little house so the Valparaiso Aero Club members and their families could stay there as needed.

Nena and her parents lived for several years in the farmhouse at Urschel Field, which had an outhouse and only one sink, located in the kitchen. Olie Sundelin and later his wife Lucy also lived in the farmhouse, as this is where they met. Lucy moved in with the Winders to get away from her stepfather, Nena's uncle. The upstairs had three unheated bedrooms. Olie's room would have snow that had blown in under the roof. Lucy became my father's (Joe Urschel) secretary, and Olie worked at Urschel Laboratories most of his life. As children we visited their home on several occasions.

Nena drew me a sketch of my grandfather's land. Beside the house was a long driveway. A large garden was in front of the house. Toward the back was an orchard and an area where my grandfather William grew some of his gooseberries. A Civilian Conservation Corps (CCC) camp was built on the property to the east of the airfield.

WOMEN WITH WINGS in Valpo

NENA WINDER   BETTE NOGARD

The conversation again returned to aviation as Nena stated that she was not close to Bette Nogard Richards, as Bette was about eight years older, but they both hung out at the airport whenever they could. As stated in the newspaper, Nena was taught to fly by her brother Bud; however, Nena refuted this. She was taught by several other pilots when the Cub was available and when they had time. To get your license, you had to complete ten hours of flying. One time Nena went up with her instructor Axel Nogard Jr. She took off and was flying around; he kept asking her to keep circling the field. She thought this was a little odd, and then he calmly asked her to land the plane. She had never landed before but did a good job. After they landed, he told her his stick had broken, and she was the only one controlling the aircraft.

Nena built up flight time, eventually logged the needed hours, and was ready to solo. She said her brother was asked to check her out; he got out of the plane, so she could fly around and land the plane. It was an exciting time for her. *The Vidette-Messenger's* front-page photo showed Nena and Bud along with the plane. The text stated that she was only sixteen years old and was the first female to solo in Porter County on July 25, 1937.

Nena spent most weekends at the airport. She and her high school best friend Betty ran a hot dog and soda pop stand to make money to support their desire to fly. As the airport was a social venue during this time, it is no surprise that Nena met her future husband Bus Babcock at the airport. After Bus and she had dated awhile, he invited her to a Sunday dinner with his family. Bus borrowed the Cub and flew them to his folks' farm. His brothers got the cows out of the way so Bus could land the plane.

Nena Winder Babcock and Cinda Urschel

When I went to Nena's for that first visit, I told her I wouldn't stay more than an hour as I didn't want to tire her. Ha! After four hours she was still going full tilt, and I was getting exhausted. What a woman! She was planning on quilting for a few more hours that evening. She makes some wonderful breads and baked goods. I could not wait for our next visit.

Nena told the story of Rollie Humphrey, who after taking a Cub out flying for the day, came back to land at Urschel Field. He turned the plane sideways and flew between the office and the hangar. He did not know an inspector was in the office with Bud Winder. She can't remember the repercussions resulting from this stunt. Rollie died in 1968 after crashing a plane in the ocean near San Francisco.

Another day a large fancy plane came to Urschel Field. Her brother Bud told her to guard the plane until the pilot returned. Although she

Left to right:
Rollie Humphrey   Nena Winder (Babcock)   Lucy Sundelin   Olie Sundelin   Bud Winder   Mabel Winder with Dixie   Dot Foster   Henry Foster

couldn't remember the kind of plane it was, she does remember lying underneath it, giving the plane her ultimate protection.

Another interesting story Nena relayed was about Bud flying his plane to be a participant in an air show somewhere east of Valparaiso. As Bud approached the field, someone on the ground signaled him to get out of there because an inspector was at the show, and he wouldn't have enjoyed seeing Bud's aerial stunts. He immediately turned around and headed back to Urschel Field.

Many pilots would gather in the hangars in the evening and spend hours talking about flying. Nena mentioned the mechanic Charles Younce as well as his pilot father William. The pilots were very close and were like brothers because their love of flying had forged a strong bond between them. Many pilots and their wives would go to the large barn on Liberty School Road on Saturday nights for dancing. Nena recalled eating and hanging out at Steve Noble's popular downtown hamburger place. Steve was a pilot in World War II and was killed in action. Another supporting member of these men was Dr. Van Winkle from Valparaiso, who would give the men and women their medical exams to get their pilot's license. Nena worked for him when she was in high school.

Lastly Nena told me about the white silk scarves. As a tradition, pilots flying in the winter with an open cockpit always wore a white silk scarf to keep them warm and prevent chafing on their necks as they were constantly turning their heads to see. The white scarves were multifunctional as they could also be used to wipe grease from their goggles.

Bud's daughter and Nena's niece, Dixie Lee Winder Terry, filled in more early Porter County history in a phone conversation in January 2013. Dixie said that as a child, she had a free run of the airport. She loved to climb up into the planes and pretend she was flying. When she was about six years old, her father Bud took her up in a plane and let her take the controls. She also commented that her father was a real daredevil in his life. He would participate in most of the air shows and could even pick a handkerchief off the ground with a stick that had a hook on it.

In 1940 Lt. Bud Winder of the U.S. Army Reserve startled the people of Valparaiso when he flew a 400-horsepower BT-9 combat plane that roared over the city. He used that plane at Urschel Field to train pilots under the defense program.

In January 1941 Bud received a second lieutenant's commission in the U.S. Air Corps after taking a six-week training course in Washington, DC. On February 3, 1941, Bud, his wife, and daughter left for Santa Monica, California. Lt. Winder began his duties as an inspector for the Civil Aeronautics Administration (CAA). Interestingly, the Federal Aviation Administration (FAA), formed in 1958, faulted pilots for doing the unsafe things Bud and his buddies had done at the myriad air shows they hosted. While in California he was also a private pilot for Frank Sinatra and other Hollywood people. Nena said she didn't fly much after her brother moved to California. She had little money and not enough to rent a plane, let alone pay for the gas.

Bud returned to Valparaiso on July 23, 1966, to participate in the dedication ceremony of the runway at Porter County Airport. Bud was the chief of the Flight Standards branch of the FAA for southern California and Arizona at this time. At the ceremony Bud stated that

> William Urschel, who provided the space for Urschel Field, was the real grandfather of Porter County. He gave me the support necessary to operate the airport and always maintained an active interest in it.[28]

In 1972 Bud retired from the Air Force as a lieutenant colonel and from the FAA in 1979.

Although their aviation experiences were different, Nena and Bud were formidable pioneers in Porter County's aviation history.

---

28. "Pioneer County Aviator Returns," *Vidette-Messenger*, July 25, 1966.

John Peksenak

February 16, 1923–February 18, 2014

John started flying in 1937 at the Hobart Sky Ranch Airport because he had friends who inspired him to learn to fly.[29] He helped build the airport and its runways. Interestingly, this airport did not have gas available to fuel the planes, and the hangar was built in the shape of an oval.

He went into the U.S. Army Air Forces, where he was awarded the Bronze Star as well as many other medals and ribbons.[30] After World War II ended, he came back to Hobart, Indiana.

In 1946 John received his pilot's license and bought a J-5 Cub Cruiser. He flew to Urschel Field many times. He said when it rained a lot, the field was like a big mud hole. He loved all the pilots at Urschel Field and especially admired Mark Murvihill because Mark had helped him with his plane.

29. Conversation at John Peksenak's house.
30. "John Peksenak Obituary," *The Munster Indiana Times*, February 21, 2014.

Norman Danielson

September 16, 1921–October 9, 1993

In October 1942 Aero Club members in the service were Norman and Kenneth Danielson, Major William Collins, Mark Murvihill, Lee Hindenburg, Fay Stringham, Roland Hardesty, Lloyd and Robert Berndt, Arleigh Johnsen, Wilson Rivadeneira, and Leo Clifford. Norman served for 3.5 years in World War II as an aircraft mechanic at Hickman Air Field in Hawaii.

Norman learned to fly at Urschel Field and worked there propping the planes, among other duties. In January 1945 he flew into Urschel Field, landing on skis for the first time. That plane had four motors. The next month he and his friend Robert Humphrey landed at Urschel Field in their Cub after wolf hunting in Kankakee, Indiana.[31]

On September 16, 1948, he received a Bachelor of Science in aviation maintenance from St. Louis University's Parks College of Aeronautical Technology, the oldest federally approved aviation school in the United States.[32]

Norman worked for many companies in his lifetime, including Boeing (as a member of the initial Boeing 747 Flight Crew Training team), Cessna, Pratt & Whitney, McDonald Aircraft, and American Air Lines. He also worked on projects concerning the SNARK missile and the F3H Demon aircraft.

---

31. "Urschel Field Tail Winds," *Vidette-Messenger*, January 22, 1945.
32. "Award Norman Danielson Aviation Science Degree," *Vidette-Messenger*, September 21, 1948.

Rolland (Rollie) Humphrey

January 9, 1916–1968

Bud Winder established an Aero Club at his field on U.S. Route 30 in 1933. Rollie and several members of this club purchased a glider.[33] Rollie was a passenger in the one-seat glider, sitting next to the pilot, Bud Winder. This was most unusual to have two people in a one-seat glider.

Rollie was one of the first members of the Urschel Field Aero Club in 1936, along with Bud Winder, Axel Nogard Jr., and Henry Foster. He received his student pilot's license in September 1936, allowing him to take solo flights. By February 1939 he had passed the flight test in South Bend, Indiana, for his private pilot's license. In August 1939 he participated in the big air show at Urschel Field, puncturing balloons draped between two poles.

Rollie was a flight instructor at the Washington Park Airport in Chicago. In 1941 Rollie became a full-time instructor at Urschel Field, and the following year he became the airport manager. Henry Foster assisted him as a co-manager.

In May 1942 Rollie left the area to be a CAA inspector for the U.S. Civil Aeronautics Administration at Meacham Field, Fort Worth, Texas, followed by being a CAA inspector for the airport in Grand Rapids, Michigan. In December 1951 Rollie was transferred to Merrill Field in Anchorage, Alaska.

In 1968 Rollie died after crashing a plane in the ocean near San Francisco.

---

33. "Rollie Humphrey Is New Manager at Local Airport," *Vidette-Messenger*, October 14, 1942.

Steven Noble
June 25, 1915–August 13, 1943

Steven was the foster son of Colba Erin and Maggie Harper Noble.[34] Steve operated Steve's Coney Island Sandwich Shop at 53 Michigan Avenue in downtown Valparaiso for several years and was assistant manager at Sandy's Lunch. He attended Valparaiso University for three years, studying engineering.

Friend Richard K. Smith recalled a time when Steve was doing work on a plane at Urschel Field.[35] One edge of a wing was lying up against the hangar. The wings were covered with canvas, and sometimes the canvas had to be replaced. Using an 18-inch needle and cording, they would sew the new canvas onto the wing. Two people were needed to push and guide the needle through the fabric.

Having learned to fly at the Winder Flying School at Urschel Field, Steve was one of thousands of Americans who enlisted in the Royal Canadian Air Force before the United States entered World War II. He did not meet the height requirement of the U.S. Army Air Forces, so this was a good alternative. Steven was in the 432 Squadron. When Steve was stationed in England in 1943, he wrote the Valparaiso Fire Department because they had sent care packages to the servicemen:

> Candy, gum, and cigarettes are a luxury here. We get 30 cigarettes a week for our ration and pay for them at that. As for candy or gum, we never see it. When a chap chews gum, he is 'up in life.' That's all to be expected here during wartime. As a

---

34. "Boys in Service Express Thanks for Packages Sent Out by Valparaiso Firemen," *Vidette-Messenger*, June 3, 1942.
35. Phone conversation with Richard Smith on January 7, 2013.

rule, I carry my own sugar along with me to the restaurants. I have yet to see a steak or eggs in London. It's on those big bombers. It will be a matter of only days before I start raids on enemy territory. I have a darn good crew. Here's hoping we see it through.

On August 13, 1943, his plane and crew went down somewhere over Germany, and he was reported missing. Approximately a third of the Royal Canadian Air Force who died have no known graves. His name is engraved at the Runnymede Memorial at Englefield Green in England. Steve was highly regarded and was one of the most experienced flyers in his command. Just before he went on his fateful mission, he received the rank of pilot officer. Fittingly, the plane flown by Steve was christened "Miss Valparaiso."

Bertha (Bette) Nogard Richards Anderson
November 10, 1913–December 25, 1986

AUGUST 6, 1940
URSCHEL FIELD DAY OF SOLO

Bette was an off-and-on resident of Porter County for 30 years. She entered the civilian pilot's training course at Valparaiso University under the Civil Aeronautics Administration (CAA) program. As a pupil of the Winder Flying Service at Urschel Field, she made her solo flight on August 6, 1940. Her brother Axel Nogard Jr. was her instructor.

During World War II she served as a member in the Women Airforce Service Pilots (WASP) program, the only woman from Porter County, Indiana, to do so. Due to the shortage of pilots when the U.S. entered the war, the WASP organization was composed of women who would fly as civilians in all non-combat stateside military missions, freeing up the men for combat duty. About 25,000 women pilots answered the call, of which 1,830 were accepted into the training program with only 1,074 passing the training. WASP members were stationed at 120 air bases in the country and flew more than 60 million miles. A woman often conducted a plane's test flight to prove the plane's reliability to the men.

Bette graduated from the WASP program on June 27, 1944. Part of her duties at Tyndall Field in Panama City, Florida, was to fly a B-26 as an air-to-air target pilot and to train gunners who used live ammunition for combat. She also flew BT-13s. Her favorite plane was an AT-6 with a 650-horsepower Pratt & Whitney engine, retractable gear, flaps, and a 2-way radio. The WASP group was formally disbanded on December 20, 1944.

After the war Bette became an instructor at Hall's Seaplane Base at Lake George, New York. In December 1947 flying the Luscombe plane she co-owned with her brother Axel Nogard Jr., she and her friend Ruth Robbins took off from Urschel Field to fly to Mexico. They both had ten days of free time and wanted to fly south. On one leg of their trip, they were near Houston and had been warned of the dense pine tree forests. The clouds were getting thicker, and eventually, they dropped to 200 feet. After realizing how dangerous it was becoming, they turned around because they had seen a ranch a few miles back. There appeared to be two runways with lots of ruts. They had a bumpy landing and taxied to the ranch house. The rancher was very surprised to see two young women emerge. He had built the runways for a Lufkin-to-Houston flying contest. They eventually landed at Brownsville Airport, the port of entry into Mexico. The next day they made it to Monterey, Mexico, where they relaxed for several days before returning to Urschel Field on January 5. More than 3,000 miles were flown, and they were in the air for more than 55 hours. Bette and Ruth never got lost as Bette believed her training in the WASP was a tremendous help.

Bette's first husband was Lt. George D. Richards, whom she had met at Urschel Field. Unfortunately, he died during World War II. George was the nephew of William and Ruth Urschel, who owned Urschel Field, where George received his pilot's license. While flying for the U.S. Army Air Forces, he was reported missing in action on October 19, 1943, during the Solomon Islands Campaign, piloting a P-38 pursuit plane. A week before he went missing, Bette set off for her WASP training in Sweetwater, Texas. She came home; however, her family and friends encouraged her to go back to her WASP training. She later married Lt. Col. Geoffrey D. W. Court and lived in England. Her third husband was Maury Anderson, whom she married in 1951. Maury was also a pilot and an employee at Urschel Laboratories, Inc.

Bette in her "zoot suit" worn for flying as a WASP in Sweetwater, Texas

It wasn't until 1977 that these women gained veteran status. They lobbied for the recognition after they read and refuted a 1976 Air Force press release stating that the Air Force was going to "start" allowing women to fly their aircraft. On July 1, 2009, the U.S. Congress awarded the WASP the Congressional Medal of Honor, which is on display at the Smithsonian.

Louis Wyckoff

May 2, 1899–October 26, 1963

Louis Wyckoff was president of the Flying Farmers of Prairie Lane.[36] The organization included farmers from Illinois, Indiana, Michigan, and Wisconsin. Louis learned to fly in a Piper Cub with Olie Sundelin as his instructor. In 1948 Louis put a landing strip and hangar on his property; consequently, he did not fly as much from Urschel Field.

On October 26, 1963, while flying into low clouds, Louis and passenger Leslie Weimer died when Louis's Cessna 182 Skylane plane crashed into Cloud Peak, which is part of the Bighorn Mountains in Wyoming. They were returning from a moose-hunting trip.

Louis's son John often flew at Urschel Field. John purchased a Taylorcraft after World War II. He also owned a Stinson and a Cessna 182 Skylane. Claude Lindberg was John's instructor. Claude was also a carpenter and built many houses in and around Valparaiso. John didn't have to pay for any of his lessons since he was dating Claude's daughter. John soloed in 1952 at age fifteen. He never got his pilot's license as he didn't like sitting in the back behind the pilot. He couldn't do his cross-country until he was sixteen, and by then flying didn't seem as appealing as it once had been. John's older brother James did fly extensively.

*Louis Wyckoff standing in his field while
Willard Rusk crop dusted*

36. Conversation with Louis's son John and his wife Jan Wyckoff.

James Read
June 28, 1933–April 4, 2022

James started flying lessons in a Piper Cub at Urschel Field when he was sixteen years old.[37] His instructor was Olie Sundelin. James recalled that Olie had a heavy Swedish accent, and he could only understand about half of what Olie said to him. They went up four times and practiced many maneuvers. Olie then told him the next time he went up, he was going to solo. James said it scared the heck out of him since he didn't understand some of the instructions. He was only sixteen and decided to quit right then and there. He didn't fly again until he joined the Navy in 1953.

His father John started flying in the late 1930s out of Urschel Field. He thinks his dad's instructor was Claude Lindberg. His father kept an Aeronca Champion, a Stinson Voyager, and a Rearwin on the field. His dad didn't fly often, sometimes only once a month. He didn't think he was in the Aero Club since he had owned his planes.

One time his dad was flying to Weir Cook Airport in Indianapolis, Indiana. His wife was in the front, and his secretary was in the back. His mom commented to his father that they had made a wonderful smooth landing. He had made a soft landing and had scraped the wing tip and broke a prop. He helped the secretary out and didn't realize his wife could not get out since her scarf was caught on the feed belt.

On one occasion his father was flying to southern Indiana and was close to Vincennes, Indiana. He was running very low on fuel and put the plane down in a wheatfield. He went up to the farmhouse and got a ride into town. He put just enough fuel in the plane to fly it to the airport, where he then filled it up.

When James was a young teenager, his father flew him to Terre Haute, Indiana. He wanted to look at a Culver Cadet that someone was selling.

37. Phone conversation on December 5, 2012.

It was a low-wing, very fast plane, and had a retractable gear. The person who was going to take them up told them he had just had a beer, and he couldn't fly. Someone else took his father up to try out the plane. After they landed, his father had the person who had consumed the beer take James up. The guy couldn't get the gear to come down for the longest time. He finally did and fortunately, they landed safely.

James highly regarded Mark Murvihill as he was a true gentleman. As part of the New Deal, President Roosevelt started the Civilian Conservation Corps (CCC). One of these camps was located on the farm of William Urschel, where Urschel Field was also located. Mark used one of the buildings from the old CCC Camp for his aircraft repair business. Most of the buildings had been torn down at the end of the war, but a few remained. In the 1940s James and a friend would ride their bikes out to hang out with Mark. He had a potbelly stove and would burn coal to keep warm in the winter. James was always amazed at Mark's ability to work outside in freezing weather without seeming to be bothered much by the cold.

1940 photo of Urschel Field with CCC camp in the upper left and farmhouse on the upper right.

James had a brother, John, who was five years older and was a doctor. One time his brother and father were flying to South Dakota, possibly to go hunting. They got up toward the Mississippi River in Wisconsin when it suddenly got overcast and very foggy. They were over La Crosse,

Wisconsin. The plane went into what is called a graveyard spiral. They were descending in a banking turn, and the turn was getting tighter and tighter. They came out in a valley and felt lucky that they hadn't hit the steep hills. They landed in a small field, and James's father didn't think he could get the plane out. They walked to a farm and were taken to the closest airport. Coincidentally, the instructor at the airport had just landed the exact type of plane and was very familiar with it, so he went to the field and flew the plane out for them.

James's love of flying was shared with others as he opened the Indiana Aviation Museum at Porter County Municipal Airport in 2000. After ten years, he closed the museum in 2010 due to the cost and the time of maintaining his planes to keep them airworthy. He also wanted to spend more time with family and friends.[38]

Some of the vintage planes in his collection:

T-34 Beechcraft trainer

1945 P-51D Mustang fighter

T-28 Naval trainer

Corsair

1952 AT-6G Texan

1957 T-34B Mentor

1943 L-2 Grasshopper

1945 F4U-5N

A-34 Dragonfly attack jet

Beechcraft Baron

1941 PT-17 Stearman

1955 T-28B Trojan

1953 DHC Chipmunk

---

38. "Indiana Aviation Museum to Close," *General Aviation News*,
    October 10, 2010.

Charles (Chuck) Hoover

November 11, 1917–March 4, 1992

In the 1920s Chuck's family left North Manchester, Indiana, and moved to Valparaiso, Indiana. Chuck graduated from Valparaiso High School and Valparaiso University with a degree in business administration.[39]

In 1940 Chuck was a member of the Civilian Pilot Training Program (CPTP) contingent at Valparaiso University and received his primary instruction through Bud Winder's school at Urschel Field. Before he left, he had about 50 hours of flying time at Urschel Field. He also participated in the Civil Aeronautics Administration (CAA) student-training program through the federal government at Valparaiso University and the Winder Flying Service. His friends said he had the "flying bug" bad.

In November 1940 Chuck was selected by the War Department for appointment as a flying cadet in the U.S. Army Air Corps. He began his training at the Spartan School of Aeronautics in Oklahoma. Four months later he received his basic flight training at Randolph Field in Texas.

In 1944 Major Hoover was awarded the Distinguished Flying Cross for his participation in the bombing mission in the North African Theater of Operations. He was piloting a P-39 type of aircraft and had volunteered to attack an enemy concentration. With two other pilots they flew through heavy anti-aircraft fire as he made repeated runs over the area, causing heavy damage to vehicles and tent areas and only leaving the area when his ammunition ran out. He also saw action in Italy and Sardinia, flew 80 missions, and downed a German Messerschmitt on February 15, 1943. The Air Medal and 1st and 2nd Oak Leaf Clusters were awarded to him by General Quesada.

---

39. Conversation on May 6, 2023, with Chuck's daughter Jackie Chester and her daughter Lynette.

In an interview with a local newspaper, Chuck made a profound remark:

> I was surprised when I returned to this country. Somehow, we at the front had received a false impression of affairs at home. We believed everyone was undergoing great hardships due to rationing and so forth. Rationing here is no hardship. Other countries have rationing, but they do not have anything to ration. America is the land of plenty. It's God's country.[40]

After the war Chuck was the manager of the Air Travel Service, a 1940s version of Uber at Urschel Field. He advertised a round trip to the National Air Races in Cleveland, Ohio. The cost was $37.50. For a couple of years, Chuck and his family lived in the little house at the airport. On many occasions when Chuck was landing at night, his daughter and wife would place lanterns on the runway and then remove them after he had landed. When Valparaiso High School would have their homecoming football game,

FLY!

See Valparaiso from the air in America's finest 4-place airplane. The countryside is now green and beautiful . . .

It's Fun To Fly !

Local flights all day Saturday and Sunday, May 10 & 11

Rates $2.00 & $2.50

**"Air - Travel"
Urschel Field**

Your Pilot: Chuck Hoover

Chuck would fly overhead and drop the football onto the field.

In October 1947 he wrote an article for the newspaper alerting the citizens of Valparaiso that he was testing several loudspeaker tests from the air at altitudes of 1,500 to 5,000 feet. He didn't want people to think they were Martians or an attack from a foreign country.

Chuck became the first pilot to use a plane as an air ambulance in

April 1949. He flew a patient from Urschel Field to a hospital in Minnesota. Another time he helped search for a couple trapped by flash floods in Phoenix's nearby mountains. He located two escaped prisoners for the Indiana State Prison in Michigan City, Indiana, and kept in touch with the police

40. "Local News Review of 1944," *Vidette-Messenger*, December 29, 1944.

over his loudspeaker. A few times people shot at the plane, but none of the bullets hit it.

Chuck flew Ray L. Villeneuve, president of Checkerway Charter Coach Company, to Kenora Airfield in Canada in October 1949. On the way they stopped in Fort Dodge, Iowa, to pick up other members of their party. They then flew the 1,000 miles to Kenora, where they hunted deer.

In 1950 Chuck, accompanied by his family, flew for Armour & Company advertising Dial Soap 50 weeks a year. They only came home to Valparaiso for two weeks at Christmas. He was flying a specially equipped four-place Navion aircraft (much like a P-51) that was sometimes mistaken

by people as a flying saucer. His idea came after his family was taking an automobile trip. He believed there were too many billboards cluttering the highways. The plane sported large signs on the fuselage panels, wing, and the tail section. His plane was equipped with 250 feet of neon tubing attached to the underside of the wings. This tubing displayed in lights a sign that read "Dial Soap—Stops Odor." That visual plus the alluring Strauss waltzes emanating from the plane garnered the attention he was looking to generate for his product.

Chuck's daughter Jackie stated that she was never afraid of flying with her dad, even if they ran into any kind of serious problems, since she always trusted him. During this time Jackie had more than 500 hours in the air, was good at handling the controls of the plane, and could talk throttle settings and altimeter readings. When Jackie was six years old, she took off from Peter O. Knight Airport in Tampa, Florida, and flew to Sarasota. She basically landed the plane herself, needing help only with the throttle because she couldn't reach it.

In 1952 Chuck was advertising Dial Soap over Portland, Oregon. He had a horrible reception from the people in that city because many citizens called the police. The people were complaining about the music, the height that he flew, and that he was doing this over their city. Hoover's reaction, reported in the Valparaiso newspaper, was as follows:

> During this time since June of 1950, I've flown over 200 cities in the United States, and never before have we had any complaints.[41]

After flying for Armour & Company for several years, the company decided not to renew his contract. They wanted to use their advertising money on television ads. He was interviewed hundreds of times on radio and TV stations and had many articles in newspapers during his travels. He and his family then settled in Valparaiso, where Chuck sold new and used planes for Aero Commander, Beechcraft, and Piper.

---

41. "Two Local Men Make News in Oregon Paper," *Vidette-Messenger*, May 5, 1952.

Carl Harvil

March 25, 1881–May 1960

Carl came to Chesterton in 1909 when he was the manager of the NIPSCO office until he resigned on September 16, 1920. He was instrumental in electrifying Chesterton. The first lighting of Chesterton was on December 12, 1909. In 1910 he established the first Studebaker automobile agency in Chesterton. In 1916 Carl and his brother Vaughn started a taxi service. At that time Carl was president of Duneland Historical Society. In 1917 he re-entered the automobile business and later sold Model Ts. In 1939 he opened another Studebaker dealership, and in 1954 he became a Packard dealer. Besides the dealerships, he owned a machine and body shop.[42]

Carl was an early flier as evidenced by his taking his seven-year-old daughter Wynona flying on July 15, 1920, from Valparaiso to Chesterton. In September 1929 Carl and his brother Vaughn were in charge of the Chesterton airfield, hoping to make it a prime landing field for Porter County.

Carl and his wife Louella adopted George Frederick and his twin brother Frederick George at age three from a Chicago orphanage that had placed a public notification in the *Chicago Tribune* that the twins were available for adoption. Carl had an American Eagle biplane at the time of their adoption, and Oakley Lutes piloted the plane that made the trip to Chicago to bring the twins home. Their birth mother was a non-English-speaking Romanian war bride. After the twins' father abandoned his family, their mother left them at the orphanage, assuming she could reunite with them after she was settled. She didn't realize the adoption was final. Their birth mother was, however, allowed to be part of their lives.

---

42. "Carl Harvil," Find a Grave, accessed November 12, 2023, https://www.findagrave.com/memorial/ 67323502/carl-h-harvil.

George F. Harvil
January 8, 1924–March 28, 2014

Frederick G. Harvil
January 8, 1924–September 10, 2012

George left and Fred right age 3

Twins Fredrick George and George Fredrick Harvil standing by their first airplane at the age of 16

George attributes his love of flying to that first plane ride at the age of three, bringing him and his brother from the Chicago orphanage to his new home in Chesterton, Indiana.[43]

At age thirteen George had an old Studebaker Rockne, named after Knute Rockne, as his father owned an automobile dealership. He would drive this car to Urschel Field and hang out. Claude Lindberg was the manager of the field then. When the twins were about fifteen years old, George and his brother purchased (for around $600) a J-3 Cub from Dr. Van Winkle, who didn't fly very often. They couldn't fly it until they received their pilot's license at age sixteen. C. Lee Nelson of Chesterton began instructing them about the plane. In 1940 they received their pilot's licenses from Claude Lindberg. They did their cross-country flights from Valparaiso to Michigan City to Laporte and then back to Valparaiso. George earned a commercial license when he was seventeen. Some of his friends and other acquaintances couldn't get their

---

43. Conversations on April 11, 2013, and April 20, 2013, with George and daughters Cindy Murphy, Kim Harvil, Carolyn Lind, and Fred's sons Fred Jr. and Tim Harvil on April 24, 2013.

licenses because spins were required, and doing them was scary—which didn't bother George.

On weekends Fred, George, Charles Younce, and Maury Anderson would help new students. It was a very busy time. Many of these students were farmers. Many farmers at that time had planes and used them for pleasure and business. He even remembered when the Bodin twins put a newly purchased hog in the back of a plane to bring it home.

Farmers were known to be stubborn and had a lot of bad habits pertaining to flying. For example, they would always try to bank way too much. Banking causes the plane to turn and lose altitude. The more you bank, the faster the turn. This can also result in the plane stalling. George always told them they were flying a little Cub, not some fancy airplane. To teach them a lesson, he would take them up to 7,500 feet and tell them to bank as usual. The plane would soon quickly start to spiral downward. They did not like this. Taking their hands off the controls, the plane would right itself. They finally understood.

George said his father Carl leased land south of the Chesterton Airport from the DeMass family for about $5 to $10 a month. The DeMass brothers used their own land and the Chesterton Airport for their planes. The DeMass field was very large with an old barn on it. George recalled that his father was not a good pilot. He would open the window of the J-3 Cub and stick his head out so he could see better when he came in for a landing. The left wing would be down way too far. He said his dad thought he just knew it all. The boys did not want their father flying, fearing he would kill himself. Carl resorted to sneaking to Valparaiso to fly the J-3. George and Fred told Claude Lindberg to revoke their father's pilot's license. Carl was furious with his sons for mentioning that to Claude.

One time George went to Indianapolis with brother Fred, Maury Anderson, and Charles Younce to buy a PT-19. The PT-19 was his favorite plane since it maneuvered well, could go fast, and made it possible for him to do a lot of stunts.

George and Fred worked for their father in Chesterton at his car dealership. At age twenty the twins purchased a 1920 UPF Waco biplane. Later, they realized it was a crazy idea to have wanted a biplane. They then purchased a Swift. The Swift was a very touchy plane, requiring expert flying skills. All their planes were kept at Urschel Field.

George and Fred were known as "the crazy Harvils," as they were frequently in trouble with the law. They even had the nerve to buzz the police station in Chesterton.

One day George flew about 180 miles to Decatur, Illinois, to visit a girlfriend. On the way back it was raining so hard he could not see the wing tips on his J-3 Cub, necessitating flying by his instruments. He finally decided to get a little more altitude and eventually was above the storm and landed safely back in Valparaiso. He said he wasn't scared but just hoped it would end well.

One time while he was flying his PT-19, he did something even he couldn't believe he did. He leaned over and pushed the button marked "Carburetor Heat." This button should never be pushed since the carburetor will freeze. Flying at 300 feet, the carburetor froze up and the motor died. He set the plane down in a farmer's field. Maury Anderson came out and got the plane. George never admitted to Maury what he had done since he would have been furious with him. He thought Maury was a very great man, very intelligent, and a really good pilot.

George sometimes flew to Johnson Beach, Indiana, and landed. The people on the beach enjoyed watching and would get out of his way. He would take off right away as he didn't want the people getting too close to the propeller.

One time at Urschel Field, a pilot landed and let his passenger out of the plane. The passenger got out of the plane in front of the struts and not behind them, which was a major mistake. He walked into the prop and they immediately flew him to a Chicago hospital. Thankfully he lived. George would always shut down his plane before letting a passenger out. He said you should never let an inexperienced person prop a plane, as it could be very dangerous.

School friends Bob and Ray Meltz wanted a ride in the PT-19. George had them wear a shoulder harness and a seat belt. George did a wingover, which was sort of a sloppy loop. While doing that, Ray took the stick and pushed it forward very quickly. The plane started bucking like a bronco. This threw George out of his seat, and the only thing that kept him in the plane was his grip on the stick. He said if that had come off, he would have been thrown from the plane. George usually wore a parachute, but on this rare occasion he was not wearing one. George regained control of the plane, landed, and gave Ray a real tongue-lashing.

George loved diving down into pastures, especially to hedgehop, where he would fly really low over the fields. One time he was flying extremely low and saw a horse in the field. He almost didn't clear the horse because this terrified animal reared just as the plane came by. George missed it by inches.

Once George decided to fly over Lake Michigan; he wasn't paying attention and flew way out into the lake. He didn't do that again because he realized if the plane developed any problems, he didn't have a close landing field.

When the twins were thirty-six years old, their father Carl passed away. George took over the Studebaker and Packard car dealerships on Fifth and Broadway, and his brother Fred managed the body shop. George quit flying in his 40s when it got way too expensive, and his wife was not too enthusiastic about his hobby, especially since he'd had a heart attack.

Fred's son Tim's most memorable Urschel Field story regarding his dad starts with George wanting to take up one of Fred's planes. Darkness was setting in, and he was told to fly a little bit and return to the field. George decided to fly to Chesterton to fly over a girl's house. Something happened and he had to land the plane. He landed it in a pasture, went to the people's house, and called Fred. Fred rolled the plane to a corner of the field and decided he would take off diagonally across the pasture. This field was surrounded by fences, and the pasture was very small. They hung a flashlight on the opposite corner, and Fred just cleared the fence as he flew out.

Both twins loved being at Urschel Field, especially enjoying all the air shows. George believes the time he spent at Urschel Field was some of the best years of his life because of the many great pilots and friends who frequented the field. When he turned 75, he was taken to the airport and celebrated the special occasion by flying in an AT-6.

Robert Harvil

July 10, 1924–October 27, 2013

BOB HARVIL

Parts Manager. Was made parts manager four years ago by Harvil Motors. Graduate of Valparaiso High School.

Robert and his family lived across the street from William and Ruth Urschel.[44] Robert's father Vaughn was very involved in early aviation. Vaughn's brother Carl lived in Chesterton, Indiana, and loved everything associated with planes and flying. They both had car dealerships.

Vaughn got interested in flying when he took an American Eagle biplane in trade for a car. He didn't know how to fly, so Oakley Lutes flew it for him. Vaughn never flew that particular plane as it required an experienced pilot to fly it.

Vaughn learned to fly at Urschel Field; his instructor was Bud Winder. Vaughn owned two Piper Cubs and kept them at the field. Robert thought the Piper was a good little plane and very affordable. The story has it that during the Depression, Vaughn flew one of his Cubs to Georgia to get sugar for his wife as he had a friend there with access to this sought-after commodity. He was also known to fly the short distance of 15 miles to Merrillville, Indiana, to get the parts needed for his auto dealership. During World War II Vaugh was in the Civil Air Patrol (CAP), which used civilian aviation resources to aid the war effort.

Robert started hanging out at Urschel Field regularly and decided that he wanted to get his pilot's license. One time when he was flying, his instructor told him to bank to the right. Robert did not perform up to the instructor's standards, so the instructor started berating Robert. Robert felt this man was yelling way too much and decided that day he would never take another lesson.

Robert told Oakley about his plans to drive midget race cars. Oakley did not think that was a good idea. Oakley told Robert that many people who were racing near his Michigan tool manufacturing business were being hauled to the hospital all the time. Robert decided not to race. Sometime

---

44. Conversations on November 8, 2012 and December 14, 2012.

after this Oakley was killed flying in the South when fog developed, and he crashed into a mountain. The Harvils were just devastated as they were dear friends with the Lutes family.

In June 1939 Robert went out to the airport after a tornado took out Bud Winder's hangar and planes. He said Bud just stood in the pouring rain in silence with tears streaming down his face. He was just in total shock. Robert loved Bud Winder and enjoyed his friendship. He also brought up the names of Bun Blackman and many of the other pilots who flew out of Urschel Field. This group of pilots and their friends often would meet together at Kenneth Urschel's restaurant in Chesterton, Indiana.

When Chuck Hoover brought his Army P-51 fighter plane to Urschel Field, everyone was surprised he could land at the airport. Robert and his cousin George Harvil slept under the plane that night and kept vigil. George owned a Waco airplane and often took Robert up and did snap rolls.

The other Harvil twin, Fred, used to fly Robert over Lake Michigan in a fixed-up PT-19 Army trainer that Fred co-owned with Maury Anderson and Charles Younce. Fred would dive down really fast toward the lake. Antics like that used to scare Robert, and he couldn't believe they survived some of the flying that Fred did.

The conversation continued as Robert told the story of a man who had been a fighter pilot who had stopped by Urschel Field. Robert was not quite twenty. Although he had been up in the PT-19 with Fred on several occasions, this time the men buckled him up and put shoulder straps and other kinds of straps on him. He wondered why they were doing this but soon enough found out. The man did a Split S maneuver and other stunts that scared Robert half to death. When a pilot does a Split S maneuver, he half rolls his aircraft inverted and executes a descending half-loop, resulting in a level flight in the exact opposite direction at a lower altitude. That night he couldn't sleep and was upset with those who had tricked him into getting into the plane. Afterward, he would not fly with anyone he did not know.

Robert liked and respected Charles Younce, who was a pilot and crop duster at Urschel Field. The Younce family lived next door to the Harvil family on Napoleon Street. Robert remembered Charles since he was about five years old. Charles' parents were Bill and Ora, and Ora did housework for Robert's mother. Bill was one of the first Aero Club members in Valparaiso.

Robert wanted to go into the service but was rejected. He had a bad eye, and one leg was shorter than the other. He learned to drive a car at the airport, taking his car out on the runway and going as fast as he could.

Eugene Clifford

October 5, 1936–December 19, 2021

Gene grew up on Campbell Street about a half mile from Urschel Field.[45] Gene would walk through the woods and a somewhat swampy area to get to the edge of Urschel Field. He started doing this when he was around five years old. He would just sit there and watch all the activity at the airport. He would only venture into the airport with his two older brothers. If an unusual plane like a biplane or twin engine came over, they would run to the airport. He and his friends built a lot of model airplanes.

While in high school Gene joined the Civil Air Patrol (CAP) for five or six years until 1957 and then joined another group called the Ground Observer Corps. Both groups were citizen branches of the United States Air Force. They did search-and-rescue missions with private aircraft owners who would volunteer their time and airplanes for training purposes. The pilots were reimbursed for the gas they used. Gene would often go up with Glen Kinneman, who owned a Taylorcraft. Sometimes an old, wrecked airplane would be taken to a certain location and hidden. They were given a certain grid to search to see if they could find the aircraft.

Gene did not get his pilot's license until he was fifty-five years old. He obtained the license through Mark Murvihill's business at Porter County Airport.

His favorite plane to fly was a Cessna 172 because he'd learned to fly in one. His least favorite was a new plane called the Light Support Aircraft (LSA) made by Cessna. The plane was designed to be flown with your left hand. It was noisy and just bare bones.

He remembers going to Urschel Field in 1950 or 1951 when he was a freshman in high school for a really big air show. CAP was involved, and a lot of barnstormers were brought in to perform. They would do stunts such as wing walking and flying in formation.

He recalled an incident that happened at Urschel Field when a very portly gentleman with an inflated ego decided he wanted to leave in the

45. Conversation on January 7, 2013.

middle of the air show, causing all kinds of trouble when he jumped into his plane and took off down the field.

Gene was the president of the Porter County Pilots Association from 2009 to 2012 and a recipient of the DaVinci Award from the Porter County Pilots Association on two occasions.

Charles Younce

October 29, 1922–April 17, 2006

Charles Younce was the son of William (Bill), who was one of the original Aero Club members in the 1930s out of Urschel Field.[46] As a barnstormer, his dad had an act, where he and his partner would fly into a field near a town. William would keep the audience occupied while his partner snuck away and changed into women's clothing. His partner would run to the plane and take off. The audience was led to believe that this unknown woman was stealing the plane.

Charles's interest in aviation was evident as a young boy. Along with his friend Robert Harvil, they built some wings and attached them to a box. They then attempted to fly off the roof of a house. Charles actually learned to fly in a glider pulled by a car his father was driving. During World War II he was in the Air Transport Command (ATC) and flew bombers from coast to coast in the United States.

After the war Charles became a flight instructor. He was twenty-eight years old when he was instructing Eugene Shipman on how to do simulated crash landings. A sudden downdraft caused the plane to flip and crash; thankfully they both survived.

Many of the men who flew at Urschel Field moved their operations to Porter County Airport in 1962. Charles Younce, Kenneth Trulock, Larry Bub, Bernie Rodgers, Lauren Uridel, Robert Housinger, and Dr. Theodore Makovsky formed the Professional Aviation Corporation to repair and maintain aircraft.

In 1962 Charles was retained at Urschel Field for crop dusting and plane maintenance. He recalled that his wife purchased him nice watches for Christmas, but she quit doing that after the DDT from crop dusting ruined them.

---

46. Phone conversation with daughter Paula Younce Carlisle and granddaughter Lisa Hobbler.

Ruth Robbins

April 8, 1908–December 30, 2010

Ruth's younger sister Marjorie was ninety-six years old at the time of our interview.[47] The Robbins family had lived in McCool since around 1825 and owned a large tract of land consisting of thousands of acres. The family was known for their Victorian home, built in 1887, which was located on Robbins Road. Marjorie stated that it had not been built with substantial materials and did not hold up in Indiana weather over the decades. The house was eventually torn down.

As a young boy, their brother Lewis would see all the planes flying overhead and would go to McCool Airport. Lewis earned his pilot's license and an engineering degree from Purdue University. He then taught Ruth how to fly. Ruth received her pilot's license in 1943 and joined the Civil Air Patrol. Ruth and Lewis were both pilots at Urschel Field and owned several planes, one of which was a Luscombe.

Culver Aug. '44

Ruth Robbins in 1944

Marjorie took rides with her brother and sister and reported that Lewis had a good sense of direction, something Ruth lacked. One time when Ruth was flying, she had to stop at many little airfields to find her way back to Urschel Field. Consequently, she always tried to fly with

47. Conversation with Marjorie Robbins Herren July 26, 2013.

someone. In December 1947 Ruth and Bette Nogard Richards flew to Mexico; thankfully, Bette had a great sense of direction. Marjorie remembers Bette and confirms that everyone liked her. Ruth eventually gave up flying because she had such a hard time finding the right field or airport.

Ruth in 1960

Vernon (Ted) Nehmelman

July 5, 1920–January 1, 2014

Ted came to Valparaiso in 1941 from Havana, Illinois.[48] Ted was a farmer and raised beef cattle while also owning Ted's Septic Tank Company in Valparaiso. He had wanted to fly since he was a little boy and was able to pursue that dream at Urschel Field with Ray Johnson as his ground instructor. Ted soloed in July 1944 and got his license from Claude Lindberg in 1945. (Claude also built Ted's house.)

Ted and his wife Josie hung out at the airport when they could. Gunnard Nielsen took Josie up for her first airplane ride in 1945. Ted purchased a Stinson airplane from Dr. Van Winkle around 1946. Together with Maury Anderson and Fred Harvil, he was part owner in the PT-19.

One day flying that PT-19, he and Josie flew to Illinois to visit relatives. They headed home when it was starting to get dark. They flew into a terrible rainstorm. Josie said it sounded like machine gun bullets hitting the plane. They could barely see and used U.S. Route 30 as their guide. As they approached Valparaiso, Ted could see the lights that had been kept on at Urschel Field.

Ted quit flying when it became too expensive.

---

48. Phone conversation on February 21, 2013.

Maurice (Maury) Anderson
December 30, 1926–January 2, 2013

Maury had been plagued by infantile paralysis and had a bad ankle.[49] In 1936 at the age of ten, an operation made his ankle more useful, but walking or running was still difficult. Maury recalled riding his bicycle out to Urschel Field when he was thirteen years old. He watched as planes flew over his house and had an overwhelming urge to fly. He took on as many of the jobs the pilots would give him. He washed the planes and swept the hangars and anything else that a kid his age was allowed to do. In 1938-39 he had a soda stand to earn extra money. He started saving his money so he could eventually take lessons when he became old enough. He fondly remembered the day when he was allowed to taxi a plane to a hangar.

When a pilot has certain limitations, he has to solo with a CAA inspector. Maury soloed in a Piper Cub at the age of sixteen in 1943. All the pilots cheered as he had overcome his severe handicaps and adversities. Maury wanted to join the military to fly during World War II, but due to polio when he was three years old, he wasn't allowed to join the service. He received his private pilot's license at the age of eighteen in 1945. He was good friends with all the pilots at Urschel Field.

In 1945 he started working at Urschel Laboratories, Inc. He loved my grandfather, William Urschel, as he thought he was very kind and even-tempered. My grandfather had invented a walking horse, and Maury stated he built the majority of it. Maury believed that William was more interested in inventing than in the business part of Urschel Laboratories.

In January 1948 Maury and Fred Harvil took off in their PT-19 (open cockpit) heading to Stuart, Florida. They landed in Orlando after flying 1,200 miles. When they left Valparaiso, they had to wear heavy sheepskin clothing since it was winter. He recalls it being really cold. They had a map and didn't get too lost or too far off course. They had to stop

49. Conversation on September 3, 2012, along with daughter Susan and wife Ingrid.

about four times for gas and to make sure they were going in the right direction. He said it was his longest flight in a plane.

Maury flew many kinds of aircraft and was a very skilled pilot. He rebuilt a Beechcraft Staggerwing and flew a Swift as well as a Fairchild PT-24. A plane he would have loved to have flown was a P-51. His favorite plane was a PT-19 that he owned with Fred Harvil. He loved the way it handled. The scariest plane he flew was the experimental Knight Twister plane, which he helped build. The first time he took it up, he thought he was going to die. The engine was too far toward the back, which made the tail very heavy. Eventually, the engine was moved up about 7 inches. He did not wear a parachute when he took it up the first time, but afterward he put one on every time he took the plane skyward. The other people involved in building the plane did not fly it. Maury was the only one at that time who was not married, so he was the designated guinea pig.

Maury performed in a few of the stunt shows at Urschel Field. Stunt flyers from all parts of Indiana and other states performed. Many people would come from all over to see the air shows. As a side business Maury would sell Cokes for 5 cents. He wanted to raise it to 10 cents but was told he couldn't, as the manager of the airport didn't think people would pay that much.

He remembers going to the site of Olie Sundelin and Bun Blackman's plane crash. Both men lived but were severely injured.

Maury flew until 1968 when it became just too expensive. The last time he landed at Urschel Field was around 1962. Since Urschel Field was scheduled to close, it had not been mowed very well, making for a rough landing. He stated Joe Urschel asked him to fly to Detroit to pick up a carbide punch press unit, as it was needed immediately.

He loved flying and thought it was some of the best years of his life. Maury was a member of the Civil Air Patrol as well as an avid sailor. Aviator Bette Nogard Richards was Maury's first wife.

Melvin Craig

June 14, 1932–December 23, 2022

The Triangle Airport in Dyer, which closed in 1965, was less than 1,000 feet from Melvin's house.[50] When he was about seven or eight years old, he started hanging out at the airport. At some point he became a "line kid," washing airplanes, mowing the field, etc. He was paid $5 once a week for doing these jobs after school and on the weekend. The instructors at the airport would also give him some flying time.

On his fourteenth birthday he took his first lesson at Triangle Airport. When he turned sixteen, he got his private and commercial licenses and purchased his first plane, a BT-13, as a senior in high school.

He later went to Urschel Field and instructed using a Luscombe plane. In the late 1940s Victor Erdelac was the manager at Urschel Field and lived in the little house at the airport. In late June 1946 Melvin and his student Wesley David from Evanston, Illinois, were involved in a plane crash on William Siever's farm. Melvin stated that Victor told him a knob had fallen off and jammed the control stick. The newspaper stated that Wesley had frozen at the controls, which Melvin refuted.

Melvin flew in and out of Urschel Field many times. He recalled that when it rained, the field was so soggy that one could hardly fly in or out of it. He knew both Willard Rusk and Mark Murvihill very well.

Melvin's career as a commercial airline pilot spanned thirty-three years. He flew for Republic Airlines, which became a part of Northwest Airlines. He owned and flew a 1963 Beechcraft Bonanza.

In October 2006 Melvin received the Wright Brothers Master Pilot Award from the Federal Aviation Administration (FAA) at Porter County Airport. The award is bestowed upon a pilot who has fulfilled fifty years of flying.

50. Conversation with Melvin on September 15, 2013.

Walter Copper, Jr.

July 1, 1924–February 2, 2015

Walter C. Copper Jr

Walter grew up in Lebanon, Indiana, where his father had owned the implement dealership, Copper Skelgas Co.[51] As a young person, Walter was fascinated with flying. He built many model airplanes and flew them in contests. When he was fourteen years old, he had a $5 ride in a Ford Tri-Motor. That was the event that prodded him to learn to fly.

Walter signed up for the U.S. Army Air Forces right after high school on July 1, 1942, in Lafayette, Indiana. Walter was a B-24 bomber pilot instructor during World War II. He was upset that he was not sent to Europe to fight and that he had to stay stateside training pilots. For 30 years he was a reserve officer, including Liaison Officer for the Air Force Academy. He was a member of the local Air Reserve in Valparaiso.

After the war Walter moved to Valparaiso in 1946 to run the Valparaiso location of his dad's business. Walter purchased an Aeronca Champion with Bernard Bowen when Bernard got his pilot's license at Urschel Field. Several times Walter leased a Tri-Pacer to fly to Chicago. In May 1953 Walter taught a class of Civil Air Patrol candidates, instructing them with the Link Trainer flight stimulator.

Mike, Walter's son, remembered that when he was in the seventh grade, Urschel Field had a bombing contest on a Saturday morning. His dad took him up in the plane with three sandbags. A barrel had been placed on the field as the target, and when they would get close, his father would yell for Mike to drop a sandbag, which entailed pushing the door open in the back of the plane and pushing out the sandbag. Whoever's sandbag was the closest to the barrel would win the money prize.

Walter would fly his daughter Sandy to Lebanon, Indiana, to visit her grandparents. After a week or so, Walter and his wife would drive to Lebanon to pick Sandy up, as her mom would not fly in an airplane.

51. Conversation with son Michael and daughter Sandy in April 2023.

Knight Twister

Vernon Payne designed the Knight Twister in 1928 while teaching aircraft design and repair at a school associated with the Aviation Service and Transport Company in Chicago.[52] The Knight Twister was sold in plan form for homebuilding. It first flew in 1932. Many pilots thought it was a very touchy airplane to fly.

In 1948 Maury Anderson, Olie Sundelin, and Art Babcock bought the plans to build the Knight Twister for $1,500. They built most of the parts in Olie's basement, necessitating knocking down a wall to get some parts out. It was one of the smallest planes in the Midwest. The fuselage measured 15 feet in length and weighed about 800 pounds. The top speed was about 160 miles an hour. It could dive at 300 miles an hour, making it a good plane for performing aerobatics. The one-place plane was powered by an 85-horsepower Continental fuel-injection engine.[53]

Maury was the first one to fly the plane because the other two were married, and their wives did not want them to fly it for the first time. He took off without a parachute. Everyone who had gathered at the field that day wondered why he was flying so fast as he almost didn't clear some trees. When he came in to land with full power, he was sweating and very white. He had to fly at full speed because the engine was set back too far. Gerald and Joe Urschel determined that the center of gravity was way off, and they figured out where to place the engine and also lengthened the nose. The second time he flew it, the engine started coming off. Debris had not been cleaned out of the gas tank. Olie and Art flew it only a few times because they were afraid of it.

---

52. "Payne Knight Twister," Wikipedia, accessed May 1, 2023, https://en.wikipedia.org/wiki/ Payne_Knight_Twister.

53. "Three Valparaiso Men Build Tiny 15-Foot Plane," *Vidette-Messenger*, November 2, 1951.

In September 1953 they participated in the first Experimental Aircraft Association (EAA) Fly-In Convention in Milwaukee, Wisconsin. There were 21 planes and about 150 participants watching the show. The EAA Fly-In grew, and this show was moved to Rockford, Illinois. By 1969 that yearly fly-in eventually found its home in Oshkosh, Wisconsin.

Maury and Charles Hoover also flew their Knight Twister to the O'Hare Air Show when O'Hare was dedicating a new runway. Hoover was supposed to fly it in the air show; unfortunately, the landing gear broke just before he was to take off, so he couldn't fly it. In 1956 Olie sold the plane to someone in Fort Wayne, Indiana, after logging more than 200 miles in it. He was told that the plane had burned in a fire due to a welding accident. He then purchased a four-place Fairchild 24.

In 2008 Bob Urschel was walking in the plant at Urschel Laboratories, Inc.[54] His eye caught a picture of a Knight Twister. The employee told Bob it was Maury's Knight Twister that was lost in a fire 50 years ago. Bob did some research and discovered the name of a man in England who now owned it. He sent emails to 25 people with that name explaining that he was looking for the plane. The next day he received an email from the man who owned it. Bob and his son Rick flew to England in January 2009. They purchased it as Bob believed that the plane belonged in Valparaiso and had it shipped to Porter County Regional Airport. Several employees

On May 19, 2009 Maury was reunited with the Knight Twister he helped build.

54. Conversation with Bob Urschel.

at Urschel Laboratories, Inc. spent weeks putting it back together. They then tied the plane down, started the engine, and propped the plane. Everyone knew they were not crazy enough to actually fly it.

On May 16, 2009, Maury and his extended family were invited to visit his plane. After 54 years apart, a most joyful Maury was lifted into the cockpit as the crowd celebrated this reuniting of a man and his plane. It was displayed at the Valparaiso YMCA for a few years and then was moved to Urschel Laboratories, Inc., where it is hanging from the ceiling in their largest conference room.

Victor Erdelac
July 5, 1922–

Victor with Stearman in 1953

As a little boy, Victor would run to the airport at 61st and Broadway in Gary to watch all of the activity.[55] Seeing planes in the sky was like a wonderful dream to him. When he was in 5th grade, the school let all of the children outside to watch as 18 to 20 twin-engine bombers flew overhead coming from the northeast and traveling southwest.

When he was fourteen or fifteen years old, he went to the Gary Airport to see an airshow. The airport was run by brothers Paul and Nick Jankovich. A pilot in the airshow by the name of Johnson did a loop in a Ford Tri-Motor. His family lived not far from the airport, but he didn't always have the money to get into a show. There was an outhouse at the edge of the woods near the field, and when someone came out and walked toward the airfield, he would get in close step behind him so that it would be like he was following his father. He loved it when a man would jump out of a plane very high up and rip open a bag of flour, as this would let the people on the ground find him in the sky before he opened his parachute. Mike Burson taught parachuting classes in the area.

Victor joined the Army Air Forces on August 9, 1941, and he was shipped to England. Being low on funds and always wanting to fly, he thought he would join the service to learn. He trained as a bombardier with one of only two heavy bomber groups in Europe as they were helping to stop Rommel from advancing across Europe. He would pull the pin on the bombs and then call the bombardier to tell him the bombs were

55. Conversations in 2015 and July 18, 2017.

armed and were ready to go. He flew 50 bombing missions and kept every pin. To identify each of the 50 pins, he put the name of the pilot, the date the bomb was dropped, latitude, longitude, and size of the bomb load on each pin. He also flew in North Africa.

Victor Erdelac, 88, of Valparaiso, displays a scrapbook containing the 50 bomb pins he pulled on B-17 missions during World War II. Next to him is a photo of Erdelac in 1945, after he returned home.

Victor came to Valparaiso in 1948 after getting his pilot's license in Florida in 1947. He went out to Urschel Field to get a job. At that time Mr. Green operated the airport. Mr. Green was tall and rather heavyset and couldn't get into some of the planes. Victor entered the office, and Mrs. Green was by herself. She told him there were no jobs available. As he was leaving, a gentleman drove up to do his first solo. Mrs. Green asked Victor if he would give him a lesson. Victor worked with him for about an hour. His student had about 15 hours of dual time but needed help with landing, as this student had not developed a glide path. Victor took him up higher in the sky and practiced gliding, as a glide has to be constant. That night he soloed him. Mr. Green then offered Victor a job.

Willard Rusk took over the management of Urschel Field, and Victor flew for him, doing crop dusting and instructing. In 1953 he crashed while crop dusting a wheat field in northeast DeMotte, Indiana. He said someone else was supposed to do the job that day. The day was very hot, and at noon he said the wind was making the wheat boil. On the south edge of the field were tall oak trees and power lines. He was halfway across the field when he felt the wheels hit the top of the wheat, and the plane flipped on its back. Victor spent many weeks in the hospital. He believed the harness saved his life, as the plane was totaled. The Indiana State Police believed the plane may have been too heavy and overloaded. On the same day as this incident, pilot Robert Hammer from Urschel Field was killed crop dusting for the Osborne Seed Co.

Victor made $4 an hour crop dusting. The first time he crop dusted, Willard Rusk stood with a long pole with a piece of cloth tied to the top to show him how to dust the rows. He always flew with a mask and goggles. The pilots were not allowed to load the chemicals. They would stand back and sometimes supervise and instruct on the loading. He crop dusted in Illinois and all the way to Franklin, Indiana, until about 1955 or 1956. He said it was challenging and fun. If the job was far away, he would sleep under the wing. They would crop dust at the crack of dawn because the wind was low at that hour. After a few hours they would wait until 4 p.m. to start again. Victor also flew out of Crown Point, Indiana, but Willard told him he was needed full time at Urschel Field.

He recalled being in a Piper Cub with a student at about 1200 to 1500 feet when out of nowhere, Maury Anderson dove close by the Piper Cub, as he wanted to give them a thrill and to show the speed of the Knight Twister.

Victor would make his students fly in the rain and with dense clouds. South Bend had the only operating tower in NW Indiana. Some of his students had a fear of using the radio. He would take them up to the tower at South Bend to hear the other pilots using the radio. He would also show his students how to fly cross-country using the beacons. Each beacon rotated Morse Code to tell the location of the beacon and what city they were in.

One of his students was "stiff as a board." Willard Rusk told him to take on this student, mentioning he would probably never get his license. This fearful student had seen a few planes without their covering and couldn't believe they were safe. Victor took him up for a 30-minute ride and did every maneuver he could think of. Teacher demonstrations followed by student practice enabled this particular fearful student to earn his license.

For a short time Victor owned a $300 Piper Cub, housed at the airport in Hobart, Indiana. He would fly it to Valparaiso to instruct students after work and then return to Hobart. One of the problems was that Hobart had no lights, and you had to land on the short field at a long angle, flying over U.S. Route 6 at night under all conditions. The engine needed costly repairs, so he decided not to fly. He gave the plane to Willard in exchange for the repair.

Victor lived and worked in Glen Park in Lake County, Indiana. He started his career as a mechanic with Grantham Motors, a DeSoto dealer, and rose to the service manager position.

As a side note, he remembers people talking about famed aviator Wiley Post landing at McCool Airport in the 1930s. He was flying a Lockheed Vega. Wiley was the first to solo around the world and developed a pressure suit that allowed pilots to fly at higher altitudes.

Victor was honored on the occasion of his 100th birthday on July 5, 2022 at the Mundelein Village Hall in Illinois. The mayor greeted him and escorted the spry centenarian to a place of honor as the color guard from the American Legion, commissioned Army officers, members of Daughters of the American Revolution, Veterans of Foreign Wars, area residents, family, and friends joined in the ceremony. Also the Northern Illinois Patriot Guard Flag unit paid tribute with their motorcycle procession. This unit represented all military branches. Following them were a contingent of Mundelein police, fire units, sheriff deputies, and three Mundelein pageant queens. Honor Flight Chicago saluted Victor with a convoy of cars and representatives as Victor was one of their first honor flights (May 23, 2012) from Chicago. Adding to the procession were a Corvette club and area classic cars. All these groups filled the field across the street from the tented seating area as they came out to personally wish him a happy birthday. North Point Digital Productions has prepared and shared several videos about Victor on YouTube.[56]

---

56. North Point Digital Productions. "Victor F Erdelac Celebrates his 100th Birthday." YouTube video, 2:31. July 6, 2022. https://www.youtube.com/watch?v=3tcnNfHokmE.

Floyd Frank
July 14, 1927–October 3, 2013

Volksplane built by Floyd Frank and Larry DeKoker

Floyd was about five years old when his father Clarence took him to Chicago Midway Airport.[57] The field was just cinder strips at that time. His father was in the Air National Guard, working sometimes as a mechanic on a World War I Curtiss Jenny biplane for Lt. Newhall. Floyd loved planes and the thought of flying. He built many model planes when he was younger. While in kindergarten in Chicago, his teacher gave him a small wooden cheese box without a top. She told him to make something with it. Floyd made a biplane, which he kept for many years.

In the spring or summer of 1947 after leaving the military in 1946, Floyd headed to Urschel Field to learn how to fly. Bus Babcock was his instructor. His first flight took him south of Valparaiso; he was hooked. Floyd took about 20 hours of instruction.

Told to do spins, Floyd and his instructor would go up to about 10,000 feet and point the plane toward the ground. Then they would let the plane do three spins. If they were flying due south before the spins, they had to end up in the same direction after the spin. They had to learn spins because some of the early planes easily went into spins.

One time when Floyd was landing at Urschel Field, he did what was called a slip maneuver. Bus Babcock had taught him how to do this. To do a slip, you would lower one wing and kick the rudder in the opposite direction. Once the high-tension wire at the north end of the runway was cleared, altitude was quickly lost so you would be closer to the runway for your landing. On what was to be the last time he was at the airport, Floyd was coming in and did this maneuver, landing safely. The fixed-base operator angrily came storming toward him. The operator told Floyd he

57. Conversations on February 5, 2013 and April 26, 2013.

95

could not do the slip landing maneuver anymore at Urschel Field because he didn't want Floyd to wreck any of his planes. Floyd tried to tell him that Bus had trained him to do this. Floyd was so mad he quit flying. He lost his pilot logbook and would have had to start all over. When he decided to go back to get his pilot's license in the 1960s, Urschel Field had closed, necessitating getting his license at the Gary Airport.

Floyd was very good friends with Fred Harvil, the son of Carl Harvil. Fred told Floyd to meet him at 23rd and Porter Avenue in Chesterton, Indiana. Fred landed in a soybean field there, and Floyd climbed into the plane. The soybeans had grown high, and the plane could not take off. Floyd got out of the plane, and Fred was then able to take off. Fred did not have a private pilot's license at that time.

Floyd was also good friends with the twins Siverd and Sylven Bodin. Floyd kept his planes at the Bodin Airport since it was closer to his home in Chesterton than Porter County Airport in Valparaiso. The first plane he kept there was a Stinson Voyager that he tied down outside. Later the Bodins told him he could use a small building on the premises for $15 a month if he would put doors on it.

Floyd was amazed at what the Bodin brothers would come up with to fix many things. They were big junk collectors and loved to find and keep all kinds of things. One day the starter on Floyd's plane wouldn't work. Siverd told him to pull the starter off, as he had an identical one that had been used on an Allis-Chalmers tractor. Directed to the second floor of the barn, Floyd went to the furthest corner, where there was a huge pile of parts. Lo and behold, he found the identical part that had been part of a tractor. Siverd installed it and had the plane back in working condition even though the starter was not a certified part.

In the 1970s the first and only complete plane that Floyd and his cousin Larry DeKoker built was a Volksplane. The maximum speed was 80 miles per hour. The controls were minimal, and it had a gas tank that held only 5 gallons. He had to have 50 hours of test flights, more than normal since it was an experimental plane. He flew it in the Oshkosh Air Show as an experimental plane. The combined weight of the pilot, plane, and anything else could not exceed 700 pounds. The plane was destroyed one day when Floyd and a very heavy iron worker caused them to exceed the 700-pound limit. Floyd was at the Bodin Airport and was taking off toward the north. He thought he was going to hit a wire and went to turn; halfway into the turn, the plane just fell out of the sky. He crashed into a soybean field and both survived.

The second plane that he started to build was the Baby Great Lakes. The wingspan was about 17 feet. Being a biplane, he would be able to do stunts in it. By this time he was in his 50s, and he started thinking about what he was doing. He had the wings built, but he decided to sell it unfinished, knowing he was getting too old. The buyer said that when he finished it, he would let Floyd know; however, Floyd never heard from him.

His least favorite plane was a Piper Arrow that he purchased in Memphis, Tennessee. He had to take several hours with dual instruction before he flew it home to a hangar at the Bodin Airport. He didn't like the feel of the tail wiggling, due to its retractable landing gear. In the winter when he took off from a snowy grass field, he worried that all the snow would freeze the gears, preventing a safe landing. He knew the possibility of this was extremely slim; but still, it always made him uneasy. He didn't keep this plane for long.

Floyd had built a Rogallo Wing type of glider. He had purchased the plans for it and built it out of bamboo, duct tape, and Visqueen plastic sheeting. At Porter Beach on the shore of Lake Michigan, they tried running down the hill with the glider, yet they never got it airborne.

Floyd rebuilt a 1941 J-3 Cub with a 65-horsepower Franklin engine purchased in 1974 from a man in Hammond, Indiana. This Cub required extensive work because it had not been flown since 1959. Screws had been used to keep the covering on instead of having the fabric sewn onto the wings. Normally, as the fabric was being sewn on, the stitcher would come up from the bottom, making a seine knot on the top. It was best when the knot was laid on top. A piece of the fabric was glued along the top; many pilots liked the knot to be just to the side of the top to give it a smoother appearance. If the knot was too far off the top, the inspector would not approve it, necessitating it to be redone.

His favorite plane was a Cessna 175 with a converted engine. His scariest flight in that Cessna happened when he was returning from visiting relatives in Florida. On the way home they ran into heavy rain. He didn't want to land at the large Atlanta airport, so he picked a smaller town that did not have a control tower. He was able to get on the correct frequency and let them know what he was going to do. Although he didn't get a response, he circled to begin the pattern for landing. On his final approach as he was getting ready to land, a plane suddenly appeared on the runway ready to take off in his direction. At that very instant his engine died. He was more scared for the other pilot, fearing a collision. He put on his landing lights, causing the pilot on the runway to see him in enough time to get off the runway. Floyd glided the plane down, coasted, and just made the runway. The other pilot jumped out of his plane and ran toward Floyd. He apologized and felt bad. That guy was the airport manager. He hadn't heard Floyd and hadn't been paying attention to incoming aircraft. They figured out that Floyd had purchased bad gas in Florida.

For many years Floyd was in charge of the Schahfer Generating Station near Wheatfield, Indiana. One time during an 8-month strike, he flew over the picket lines and a 138,000-volt power line to land on a 1,400-foot road near the ash pits. His plane was shot at, and water was put into the gas tank during this time. His wife then hired armed guards to protect their house.

Floyd built a home at 5th and Porter Avenues. This was the property the Chesterton Airport occupied at one time in 1925. When digging for a swimming pool, they found the foundation of the old barn. This was the barn that had been somewhat converted into a hangar back in the 1920s.

Charlie Comer

April 4, 1931 –

Charlie took his first lesson at age fifteen and received his student license at the Medaryville Airport.[58] The cost was $6 an hour for solo time and $8.50 with an instructor. The Medaryville Airport closed around 1947, having been open for only three years. He earned his private pilot's license at the then Hammond-Chicago Airport (renamed Lansing Airport in 1976) at the age of eighteen in 1949.

One day he took off on his first cross-country solo. He left from the Hammond-Chicago airport heading to Kankakee, Illinois, and then on to Rensselaer, Indiana. A fog grew heavy, diminishing visibility on his way to Rensselaer and making for a scary trip. He knew his location when the fog came. He started flying at treetop level, and using a compass, he found the Monon Railroad tracks that would then lead to Rensselaer. The airport was about 1.5 miles from the tracks, and he estimated the approximate time that each event would happen. As luck would have it, the fog lifted a little, and through a hole in the fog, he spotted the airport and landed. "Cross-country" meant anything over 30 miles, and "IFR" meant, "I Fly Railroad," instead of instrument. He went to Medaryville, spent the day with his father, and later in the day flew to Chicago.

Charles always wanted to learn to fly. He and his best friend Sam Antiona would have loved to have flown in World War II, but they were way too young. They would see pictures of the pilots in magazines and dream of wearing a uniform and having wonderful mustaches. Sam grew a mustache in high school, and Charlie told him it looked horrible. The reason he told his friend this was that he was jealous because he was unable to grow a sufficient-looking mustache.

58. Conversation on December 21, 2012 at Urschel Laboratories, Inc.

Charlie later joined the Air Force and got out in March 1956. He owned a 1943 Fairchild PT-19 at this time and kept it at a private field in San Pierre, Indiana. He and Sam both wanted to make a career in aviation. They both lived in Medaryville and would come to Valparaiso to fly.

In 1956 they both earned their commercial and multi-engine licenses at Urschel Field. Their instructors were Willard Rusk, Keith Baird, and Charles Younce. Much of his training was in a Cessna T-50, which was constructed of tubes, fabric, and wood; it was also known as the "Bamboo Bomber." He started logging miles for his commercial license first; then while getting that, he started the certification process for his multi-engine license. It became too confusing, so he finished his multi-engine first and then completed his commercial license.

He started working at Urschel Laboratories, Inc. in 1959 and finished both licenses at Urschel Field. He and his friend Sam went to Kansas City to interview to become commercial pilots with United Airlines. They were told they were qualified; however, they were not accepted into United's program. They needed to increase their hours of flying. Becoming a commercial pilot was their ultimate dream, and they both added many hours of flying time. Some of the additional hours required for the airlines were hours attained in night flying. He and Sam would fly many times to Urschel Field during the winter. Every time they would land at night, they would spot two little heads peeking at them from the north end of the runway in the snow bank. Eventually, he asked the thirteen-year-olds if they wanted to go on a plane. Of course, they did, and off they soared into the sky.

He started working on his instrument license. The school was in the north hangar and had a Link Trainer flight simulator that you sat in. You could bank and pitch; it would turn in a complete circle. The term "Link Trainer" is commonly used to refer to a series of flight simulators produced between the1930s and early 1950s. They became famous during World War II when they were used as a key pilot-training aid by almost every combatant nation. This equipment provided a safe way to teach new pilots how to fly by instruments. He had spent only two hours in the Link Trainer before the hangar burned to the ground.

Of the infamous hill on the north end of the Urschel Field runway, Charlie said that when you came in to land, you would do a flare. The problem was the hill would disappear, and you would still be 20 feet in the air. You needed to let the plane float and then land.

Concerning other features of Urschel Field, Charlie recalled that the south hangar at Urschel Field housed the planes of private owners; the north hangar held a lot of Willard Rusk's business planes. Charlie was a very good friend of Willard Rusk and mechanic Bernie Rodgers. Bernie's photo of the airport in 1955 did not show the maintenance building in front of the office, but it was there in a 1956 photo.

1955 photograph of Urschel Field.

Charlie and Sam finally gave up their dream of flying for a commercial airline. As Charlie definitively exclaimed, "Enough is enough!" The airlines always upped the hours every time they went for interviews. They had spent a lot of money to qualify, and they both came to the conclusion years later that they were just not tall enough.

Charlie owned a 1949 Piper Clipper and later an Engineering and Research Corporation's 1948 Ercoupe, which he flew out of Rensselaer, Indiana. His favorite planes were a PT-19 and a Cessna T-50. He always wished he had flown a P-51.

Andrew Royko Jr.

November 28, 1933–February 13, 2022

The first thing Andrew mentioned was that he hated landing at Urschel Field if you were flying in from the north.[59] A 20-foot drop was required because of the hill. (Different pilots give much different measurements.) A good strong wind coming in from the south would keep you aloft with little runway left, requiring giving the plane gas, circling, and trying again. Through the years he landed at Urschel Field 25 to 30 times and once even left his plane there to be repaired. He enjoyed and respected all the pilots. Everyone was always giving a helping hand to anyone who needed something done on their planes.

A farmer who flew a biplane taught him to fly. Andrew did not remember his name but did remember that his license cost him $14. His brother Joseph had a Piper Cub, and Andrew, too, bought his own for $150, eventually selling it to a man named Hamilton at Porter County Airport for $300. He earned money by helping a lot of the farmers with various tasks. He felt planes were relatively cheap back in those days and would have loved to have flown a B-21. Andrew served in the Army's 101st Airborne Division.

His plane was kept at a field located at Mineral Springs and Old Porter Roads in Porter County, as his father owned a farm next to this field. He thought the railroad owned the land where the field was located. At any one time 20 to 30 planes were parked at the field. His dad would allow the pilots to tie down their planes. In turn they put up hay, fixed the tractors, and performed various other farm chores. The pilots came from Valparaiso, Kouts, Hebron, Michigan, and Illinois.

Sometimes his father would get angry with the biplane pilots when they would fly too close to his barn. Many were World War I pilots. He swears that some of the biplanes were kept together with baling wire. On the weekend they would have air shows at this field. The cars would be backed up for miles to get to the field. He said it would have been marvelous if a movie had been made as many people would not believe all the stunts the pilots did. For example, a pilot would swoop down, slap the large oak tree on the east side with a wing, and then land. There were no regulations in the early days. He was always amazed that he never

---

59. Conversation with Andrew on May 1, 2013.

once saw an accident in all of those years. If the pilots needed gas, they would go to the old Martin station on U.S. Route 20 and get regular gas for their planes.

Andrew recalls Carl Harvil flying out of the field in a red biplane. Some of the pilots told him not to take off one day. Rain had rendered the field a muddy mess. Well, he hit a rut and flipped the plane, wrecking it. The propeller was broken, and the tail was badly damaged.

Many of the pilots would take Andrew up for rides. When he was about twelve, one of the pilots took him up and did all kinds of spins, loops, and the death roll. He got very sick to his stomach. After landing, he was weaving as he walked. His mother was in the garden working and was furious; she yelled at the pilot. "I told you guys not to take Andrew flying. Now look at what you have done. He has work to do, and you have messed that up!"

On some occasions the pilots would land at Brassie Golf Course in Chesterton, Indiana, where the land was level. They would pick up their friends and fly off to different places.

Andrew never kept a logbook, but his last flight was with his brother-in-law Everett Berndt, who owned a Stinson. They were coming into Porter County Airport, and half of the fabric flew off the plane. They had to hold the right rudder down and were scared they weren't going to make it to the airport. That was the last time either of them flew.

James (Jimmy) Walsh
April 10, 1926–March 29, 2019

Jimmy starts at the very beginning, telling the story of his entrance into life.[60] His mother was just starting labor. The doctor had been at their house and told everyone that it would be 12 hours or more. Everyone left, and within an hour she had given birth to Jimmy all by herself. Her neighbor came back and was amazed the baby had been born.

While in high school, Jimmy was good friends with Johnny Fetla. Once a week in downtown Valparaiso, they would have wrestling events. Johnny and Jimmy would put on a wrestling show before the big main event. They were paid 50 cents to do this. They also worked at the Hotel Lembke washing windows and would help the maids clean the rooms. He was paid 50 cents for working about four hours at the hotel.

Jimmy's father started working at Urschel Laboratories in the 1930s; Jimmy started there in about 1946-47, retiring in 1987. Maury Anderson and Olie Sundelin also worked at Urschel Labs. At that time it was located on Napoleon Street. They encouraged Jimmy to fly because he often rode his bicycle out to the airport to watch all the activity.

During World War II he wanted to join the Navy since he liked to swim. He did not want to join the Army or Marines. He used to watch them march through Valparaiso and did not want to ever have to do all that marching. He didn't finish high school because he didn't want to get drafted into the Army. He joined the Navy at seventeen and off he went.

Using the GI Bill, he started taking flying lessons at Urschel Field, receiving his pilot's license in the early 1950s. His ambition was to have a business flying fishermen and hunters to Canada, which was a very lucrative business to be in at that time. He was married in 1955, and the

60. Conversation November 7, 2012, with Jimmy and Carol.

GI Bill ran out for him. The government determined he was not as serious as they thought he should be about his plans for this new business. He did not fly as often as he wanted to. He did not own a plane, so he would rent, usually a Cub, from Rusk Flying Service.

One day Willard Rusk called Jimmy and wanted him to come to the airport. A Hammond, Indiana, man had called Willard, wanting a favor. This man, who was an instructor, would come to Valparaiso and then fly to South Bend, Indiana, for business. He realized that he if took a GI Bill student, the trip would be paid for by the government. They took off following U.S. Route 30, heading for South Bend. Jimmy was told that this man needed a few minutes in South Bend, but the few minutes turned into a few hours. When they were in the air on the way back, they ran into really heavy fog. They couldn't see U.S. Route 30, so they turned north. They found U.S. Route 20, watched the lights of the cars peeking through the fog, and made it to the State Police Barracks on Indiana State Road 49. From there Jimmy knew how to get back to Urschel Field. Much to his relief, the oil pots were still burning. Urschel Field was lined with oil pots, as this was before the airport obtained lighting for the runway. He barely knew how to fly a plane in the daytime, let alone at night. He said it scared him so much that he never flew at night again.

One day he wanted to do some flying. He was watching a plane coming in to make a landing. He pulled his plane to the side so the incoming plane could land. On the back of the Cub was a tail skid that kept the back of the plane off the ground. As Jimmy started down the runway, this tail skid got caught on something. The plane was trying to move forward but was being held back. He exited the plane and lifted the tail up and off of what he thought was some kind of vegetation. Well, the plane started down the runway without him. He said he never ran faster in his life and caught up with the plane and jumped in. By now he was halfway down the runway and had to turn around and start over. He was mortified since he thought other pilots had seen this, and he didn't want to land and be ridiculed by the guys. He kept flying until he had to land due to a lack of fuel. He was relieved to find out that no one had seen what he had done.

His father taught classes at the Civilian Conservation Corps (CCC) camp near Urschel Field and instructed students on how to run lathes and drill presses. He and his father would walk there because they lived on Campbell Street behind St. Paul's Church. You had to be seventeen to join the CCC. One time the boys from the camp planted hundreds of trees in the median on a street in Valparaiso. They were a total traffic hazard—many cars were hitting them; consequently, the trees were removed.

The person that he remembered especially well was Cliff Magnor. He stated that Cliff just lived for the airport and was there whenever he could be.

Anthony (Tony) Campolattara

September 26, 1917–March 22, 2010

As a young boy Tony built a lot of model planes.[61] While living in Chicago in 1933, he heard a loud noise and rushed to the roof of the apartment building. The sky was very overcast when all of a sudden, the Graf Zeppelin appeared out of the clouds. He was just thrilled to see the Graf Zeppelin as it was making a world tour.

His family moved to Valparaiso in 1947. Tony would go to Urschel Field to get aircraft dope from Lawrence "Mark" Murvihill to use on his model planes to make them airtight.

Charles Younce encouraged Tony to learn to fly. He took his flying lessons at Urschel Field, soloed on November 9, 1952, and earned his pilot's license on September 22, 1953. His instructor was H. H. "Bud" Wait. He used a Taylorcraft to do much of his training.

Tony told Mark that he wanted to purchase a plane. Mark bought a 1951 L2M Taylorcraft for $40 from Ernie Schube in Crown Point, Indiana. The plane was a mess, but Tony and Mark rebuilt it together.

His working career began at gas stations and auto dealerships. He and his brother decided to open their own station after he had worked at the Lincolnway Highway Garage. Tony's son Guy said his dad was one of the first people who could work on automatic transmissions. He owned Tony's Auto Service from 1958 to 1979.[62]

Guy drove me around the Urschel Field area and showed me exactly where both the N-S and the E-W runways had been. He said there were threshold lights at each end of the N-S runway. These were green, and there were three on each side at the ends of the runway. White runway lights lined the whole length of the runway, spaced every 100 feet or so.

---

61. Conversation with son Guy Campolattara.
62. "Valpo man loved to fly," *NWI Times*, May 14, 2010, accessed July 21, 2023, https://www.nwitimes.com/news/local/obituaries/valpo-man-loved-to-fly/article_4ed3fbd5-dd27-5773-94a7-10bccdd872ff.html.

Bernard (Bernie) Bowen

October 24, 1921–May 16, 1979

Bernie's family lived on Roosevelt Road in Valparaiso, Indiana, across from where Thomas Jefferson Middle School is now located.[63] His home was just a few blocks from Urschel Field. As a small boy watching the planes fly over his house, he decided he wanted to fly. For many years going to the airport was his favorite pastime.

In June 1946 Bernie was awarded the Bronze Star Medal by the Commanding General, Fourth Infantry Division at the direction of President Truman. Bernie served in the Army for 5.5 years with 18 months of that in Europe.[64]

Bernie learned to fly at Urschel Field in the early to mid-1950s; his son Roger thinks this was made possible only by the GI Bill. Besides being an instructor, he fixed airport radios and put skins on airplanes. He co-owned a Piper Cub with Walt Copper and later purchased a Stinson. He would bring home disassembled planes and apply aircraft dope to them in his garage.

Bernie sometimes would fly his family to Covington, Indiana, to visit relatives. Bernie and Roger often would fly locally. Roger stated his father never showed fear. Roger's mother rarely flew with her husband Bernie because she was a little scared of flying since it was relatively so new.

On May 2, 1959, Bernie, as the pilot of his Stinson with three passengers, took off from Urschel Field with plans to fly to Purdue University, where James Deck, one of his passengers, was to add a class to his aeronautical engineering schedule. His other passengers were Gerald T. Barta and Robert Quear. Bernie claims that after a good takeoff and reaching 200 feet, the engine's carburetor iced in the high humidity. Realizing the plane was too low to make it back to Urschel Field, he tried to avoid the houses and the high-powered utility lines. He bounced across the rough field, hit a fencerow, and overturned. With the men hanging upside down, the plane immediately caught fire, but all managed to escape; Deck had to be cut from his seatbelt by his friend Barta. Deck suffered severe back injuries. The fire department could not do anything, and the plane was destroyed. The accident happened across from Bowen's and

---

63. Conversation with his son Roger Bowen in 2013.
64. "Looking Backward: Ten Years Ago," *Vidette-Messenger*, June 22, 1956.

Deck's homes. The insurance company would not pay for the damage; they believed Bernie was buzzing the houses and not flying safely. Deck also told his mother he didn't believe there was any engine trouble. Roger believed his father never piloted a plane again after this accident, and if he did, he did not disclose this to his family.

Bernie owned Valpo TV Clinic on Michigan Avenue and a Pure gas station close to Porter County Airport.

Sylven Bodin

February 19, 1914–April 10, 1989

Siverd Bodin

February 19, 1914–January 24, 1984

Most of what was known about the Bodin twins came from an interview with Wally Cox, who knew them quite well. Wally had been a master mechanic at Bethlehem Steel.[65] In the 1950s one of his friends who knew the Bodin twins introduced them, and they became like father figures to him. He would often come to Urschel Field with the Bodin brothers, and they often flew together. Wally got his license in 1967 at the Gary Airport, as Urschel Field had closed by that time.

Wally liked Urschel Field and the people who were there. He also mentioned the Harvil boys, Fred and George, remembering they used to fly really low over Chesterton in their BT-13, which ran on tractor fuel.

The Bodin twins were known to harass everyone at the airport. They also never thought twice about going into a bank with their big boots covered in manure even though they knew it would aggravate everyone else.

In 1948 the Bodin twins built Bodin Airport on their farm near County Road 1400 North with IN-70 as its identifier. Initially, the airport field was on the east side of the hangar they built. That land was usually wet, so they moved the field to the west side of the hangar in 1952. It had a 2,500-foot runway that was lighted. They owned an Aircoupe, a Cessna 170, and a Cessna 180.

Both Bodins were very involved with the Flying Farmers and flew with them on many occasions. Siverd participated in the "People to People" tour in South America, a 21-day goodwill tour to see other agricultural practices.

Sylven was married and worked at U.S. Steel while also helping out on the farm. Siverd never married and was mainly a farmer; however, he flew more than Sylven. Siverd served on the Porter County Airport Board for many years.

The brothers were involved with a grapefruit and tangerine grove in Texas that was owned by an elderly man. When that man was ready to sell, the twins were able to buy it for next to nothing. The Bodins eventually

---

65. Conversation with Walter Cox on June 30, 2013.

gave the grove to a hired hand who had looked after the grove for them when they were not there.

One time the Bodins went to a sale and purchased 12 tombstones. They brought them home and lined them up near an old shed that was near the house. It looked like a real cemetery, and many thought it was.

One day Sylven was at Porter County Airport when an airplane from Uruguay arrived. The men were here on business and needed to have work done to their plane. They followed Sylven to his airport on the farm, where Sylven fixed the problem in his machine shop. The men owned a sugar beet farm and plant in Uruguay. They became acquainted that day, and Sylven and his wife were invited to South America, where they stayed for a month. Sylven would fly down there and help the farmers with equipment, using the knowledge he had acquired as a farmer.

In 1954 there was a story about a pig who went to market. The Bodins flew to Peoria, Illinois, and purchased a 200-pound Yorkshire boar that they intended to breed. They flew back to their farm in a Cessna 170 with the pig in a crate at the back of the plane.

Valparaiso contingent at a dinner club in Cuba. Photo provided by Betty Ann Johnson Troop. Right front to back: Jeanette Switzer, Ruth Dreessen, Mary & Ray Johnson, Ben Kosmatka, Sylven & Edna Bodin. Left front to back: Willard & Barbara Rusk, Harley & Lois Dowell, Paul & Mary Black, Emil & Virginia Beeg.

Ray Miller told a story about the Flying Farmer trip to Havana, Cuba, for their convention. On March 17, 1956, Sylvan and his wife flew from Valparaiso to the Tamiami Airport in Florida in his Cessna 170. This airport had been established in the mid-1940s and was located southwest of Miami. One hundred other planes from all over the United States joined them at the airport. They were then escorted to Cuba by the Cuban Navy and the United States Coast Guard. It took two hours and seventeen minutes. They returned to Florida one week later. Three other planes with 12 occupants from Valparaiso also joined them on the trip.

Separately, Siverd flew his Luscombe 8E to Key West and then on to Cuba. Batista was in power at this time. Siverd, being Siverd, came dressed in his coveralls, sported farm boots, and carried his clothes in a burlap bag. The convention was at a beautiful, very expensive hotel. Everyone else was dressed to the nines. Well, Siverd walked up to the desk and asked for his room. After looking him over, the clerk told him he didn't have a room. They finally found his reservation, but even the bellhop was not willing to touch this so-called gunny sack until Siverd insisted on help getting to his room.

In 1950 the brothers applied for a patent for a soybean combine that Siverd had designed and Sylven had built. The whole process took seven years from start to finish. Attending many farm shows enabled them to pick up materials to help with their many ideas.

Leland Gaines

October 5, 1918–June 13, 1997

LELAND GAINES

Leland learned to fly at Urschel Field.[66] In January 1951 Leland had about five hours of solo time working toward his pilot's license. When he started his lessons, he purchased a two-place Cub. Leland also owned a 140 Cessna N43. According to his son, the plane is still in service in Alaska as a bush plane.

Leland was a farmer in Boone Township and belonged to the Indiana Flying Farmers organization, serving as vice-president in 1967. That year more than 100 Flying Farmers arrived in Valparaiso for their spring meeting. His mother Doris once held the honor of being named Indiana's Flying Queen.

---

66. Conversation with son John Gaines.

Cliff Magnor

March 27, 1934–

Some of Cliff's earliest memories are of living in a rented home in Beverly Shores, Indiana, for a year while his father, a steel-mill foreman, and his father's brothers built their home on Spectacle Lake in time for him to start at Cooks Corners School on Campbell Street in Valparaiso.

When Cliff was six years old, his family drove to the Gary Airport, which had a grass field at that time. That particular day pilots were giving people rides in airplanes. He took a ride with his father in a Curtiss Condor 18-passenger airplane. The plane was full as they flew over Gary at dusk. All the lights came on, and Cliff always remembered what a beautiful sight it was. The plane's pilot was the famous barnstorming Clarence Chamberlin, who flew across the Atlantic two weeks after Lindbergh and piloted the first transatlantic passenger flight across the Atlantic.

When he was in the third or fourth grade, Cliff would walk to Urschel Field on weekends and during the summer. Helping the pilots with small things, they sometimes would take him up for a ride. Many planes didn't have engine heaters, and when it was really cold, the airport activity was minimal. Sometimes he would play ping-pong in the office. When Cliff graduated from grade school, he was given a choice for a gift. He could have a phonograph player or an airplane trip to Tennessee. Of course, he chose the airplane trip and flew on an Eastern Airlines DC-3 from Chicago Midway to Louisville and then on to Tennessee. The pilot of the plane was Robert Lewis of Valparaiso. Coincidentally, Cliff met him a few years later at Urschel Field.

When he was about thirteen, Chuck Hoover hired him at 50 cents an hour to do work around the airport such as wiping down planes with kerosene. Chuck was a hero fighter pilot in World War II who later sold planes for Eli Graubart and did aerial advertising.

Cliff mentioned farmer Claude Lindberg as being the manager of Urschel Field in 1943, followed by Earl Green, Rollie Humphrey, and then Willard Rusk. Claude trained Cliff using a two-seater side-by-side all-metal Luscombe plane. One day when Cliff was about fourteen or fifteen, he told Claude he was curious about how a spin would feel in an airplane. Up they went in the Luscombe, making three rotations. The Luscombe would lose about 800 to 1,000 feet with each rotation. Cliff didn't think he could ever learn to do that and thought maybe he should quit having any dreams of flying.

When Maury Anderson flew the Knight Twister for the first time, Cliff recalled a mild argument regarding who was going to take it up. One or two of the wives told their husbands not to go first. Maury was the only unmarried pilot, so the honors went to him. Cliff, along with a few spectators, watched that first flight. Maury took off northbound on the runway, flew only once around the airport, and landed at the south end heading north. Terrified, Maury had to fly the whole time with the stick at full forward to keep the tail up.

In 1950 Cliff soloed at age sixteen. It was a warm spring day, and he flew around the airport three times in a bright yellow Piper J-3 Cub. That same year in Dowagiac, Michigan, he bought his first plane, a 1946 J-3 Cub advertised in *Trade-A-Plane* for $495. He also purchased a 1937 Studebaker Dictator car for $175. He paid cash for both from his airport wages. As he got older, he earned 60 to 70 cents per hour. He earned some of his money mowing the runway using a tractor that had two big rear tires. The mower blade was attached to a side bar that was only 5 feet wide. The longest runway was 2,600 feet long by 200 feet wide, requiring many days to mow it just once.

When Cliff was seventeen years old, he went to Michigan City, Indiana, for his private pilot's license. The FAA inspector who qualified him was

Joe Phillips. Qualifying included flying, performing prescribed maneuvers, and passing written and oral exams. He flew over in his Piper J-3 Cub; he recalled that gas cost about 40 cents a gallon. A few days after getting his license, he flew his supportive mother around the Valparaiso area as his first passenger in a Luscombe. Cliff was the only student in his high school who was a pilot, making him quite popular. For example, he flew a date and another couple to the Indianapolis 500 flying a Stinson (Flying Station Wagon) that had wood paneling on the inside and a reinforced floor. Cliff would sometimes fly his dates to Lake Michigan in a J-3 Cub which had big, soft balloon tires. They would land on the beach, swim for a while, get back in the plane, and fly back to Valparaiso.

Four or five transcontinental train tracks converged south of Valparaiso, near Wanatah, Indiana. These trains traveled 50 to 60 miles per hour. Cliff, flying his J-3 Cub, would touch down on the back of a boxcar, sit on the top of it for a minute or two, and then lift off. This was done only on freight trains. Wendall Stoner, using his own plane, sometimes would join Cliff in these antics.

In 1952 Cliff sold his Piper J-3 Cub for $20 less than he originally paid. As a member of a plane club, he then bought into a 1947 Piper PA-12 Super Cruiser, which was kept at Porter County Airport in a T-hangar because at that time, Urschel Field did not have this type of hangar. Porter County Airport was preferred because it had a paved runway rather than muddy fields, and its lights were kept on all night. At Urschel Field kerosene lanterns were secured in concrete blocks. At the prearranged time, these portable lights would be hauled out, lit, and then removed after the flight landed. One time Bud Wait landed on a light, resulting in a big hole in the bottom of his plane.

Cliff and his fellow pilots would fly in formation over Valparaiso on the weekends to stir up interest in the airport. They flew at 1,000 feet, which was the lowest legal height. A typical weekend at Urschel Field would have 30-plus planes taking off and landing. People came from all over. He remembers a furniture store owner from Michigan who would often fly in with his Cessna Sky Master. Sometimes they would have a dance in one of the hangars, which would be cleared out and decorated for the occasion.

When Cliff graduated from high school, he worked at the steel mills in Gary, Indiana, while still mowing the runways for Willard Rusk and doing other odd jobs. He earned his commercial rating at age eighteen and at nineteen did his first parachute jump in Cedar Lake, Indiana. Cliff and a friend decided to enroll in the Lewis School of Aeronautics in Joliet, Illinois, where they shared a sleeping room. Cliff was in school from 8 a.m. until 2:30 p.m. and then worked from 3 p.m. until midnight in a diesel-train-engine factory. Exhausted, he did not complete the course but came back to Valparaiso to earn his A&E (aircraft and engine) mechanics certificate from Willard Rusk.

In 1954 with the draft going on, he went to Chicago for the physical, written, and oral tests to become an Air Force cadet. Although he passed, he followed the advice of the many World War II pilots at Urschel Field who cautioned him that if he went into the Air Force, he would have to commit to four years and one month. He may get 600 hours of flying, but he would fly aircraft that would be inconsequential in his quest to become a test or airline pilot. He was drafted into the Army 30 days later for a two-year commitment, stationed at the Panama Canal. Some of the employees at the base in Panama had their own planes. One man who didn't know how to fly owned a four-place Stinson Voyager. Cliff often had the opportunity to fly his plane.

Upon returning home from Panama, Cliff studied aeronautical engineering at Indiana Technical College in Fort Wayne, Indiana, because this program was 27 months versus 4 years at Purdue University. While in Fort Wayne he lived and worked at a large funeral home, doing a variety of jobs in the funeral home business. His grandfather had been in charge of a cemetery, so the funeral business did not bother him.

Cliff's friend Kenneth Marsden learned to fly at Urschel Field from Willard Rusk. Kenneth opened an aviation business, including a maintenance shop, flight school, and Aeronca Champion distributorship at Smith Field north of Fort Wayne. Cliff was recruited to work full time at his friend's business while earning some of his licenses there, including multiple-engine, flight instructor, and instrument rating. Cliff did most of the work at this company and began thinking about ways to accelerate his career. Test pilots from Wright-Patterson Air Force Base would come to Fort Wayne to be in the air shows and races after these were relocated from Cleveland. In talking with them, Cliff finally decided that he did not want to be a test pilot because it would not be steady work during times when a company did not have any new planes on its drawing board. Flying for the big airlines was starting to appeal to him.

Governors Air Park in Chicago Heights, Illinois, needed a pilot to fly a twin-engine plane for a gas and oil company. They eventually upgraded to a Cessna 310. Cliff flew this over much of the U.S., including Wyoming, Texas, Kentucky, Missouri, and Florida. If he flew a family to a location for an extended vacation, he was given the company credit card and could fly the plane wherever he pleased. He came to Valparaiso often to visit his parents and everyone at Urschel Field.

Cliff had many stories to share about the early days of aviation in Northwest Indiana, one of which was the big rotating beacon at McCool Airport in Portage, Indiana. Its green light indicated a landing field and was also a helpful reference point for night flyers, especially student pilots heading back to Urschel Field from Chicago. He used a 16/16 box camera, and today Cliff has a photo collection of Urschel Field, including photographs taken from the air. He also mentioned following the 20th Century Limited train in his plane. He had the opportunity to ride on that special train from New York to Chicago after his stint in the Army.

Cliff knew the Bodin brothers and related a humorous story about them. They dressed as they pleased, usually looking rather scruffy. Eli Graubart, one of the biggest used-plane dealers in the United States, started at Ravenswood Airport in Illinois, eventually moving his operation to Porter County Airport in Valparaiso. Sometimes he had 200 to 300 planes to sell. The Bodins decided they wanted a double-engine plane and went to see Eli, who decided not to sell the two scruffy men a plane that he didn't believe they could afford. They got mad and went to Chicago to buy their plane. They couldn't wait to show Eli their paid-in-full cash purchase.

When asked about Irene Leverton, Cliff didn't really know her but remembered that she had crashed a Super Cub airplane. Willard had told all the pilots that crop dusters should never look back when they are dusting. They would fly about 70 to 80 miles per hour over the crops because of the heavier load of chemicals. They flew about 10 feet off the ground. The corn could be 6 to 8 feet tall, and they couldn't fly lower because of the landing gear and the boom going out on both sides of the plane with the spraying nozzles. Well, Irene took her eyes off the crops and crashed, flipping the plane upside down. She wasn't hurt, but the plane did not fare as well.

Cliff knew the Harvil brothers very well, as well as their car dealership and repair garage in Valparaiso. In the back of the repair shop was a fully assembled airplane tilted on its nose so that it would fit. He thinks it was a J-3 Cub. George and Fred removed parts from the plane and then reassembled it in the back of that garage.

As a teen Cliff very much wanted to know what it felt like to fly upside down, so he approached Fred Harvil offering to wash his PT-19 plane if Fred would take him up and fly upside down. Fred obliged, doing a snap roll while making a wide turn around the airport before landing. Cliff thought what they had done was just fantastic.

Cliff had only one engine failure while flying. He was close to Urschel Field and was able to glide the plane safely back to the airport. He loved flying the J-3 Cub with the doors open; he remarked that you couldn't hear anything, but it sure was fun.

Still involved in aviation as an instructor at National Flight Simulator in Manchester, New Hampshire, Cliff has an H-model Beechcraft Bonanza but does instruction in a Piper Cherokee. Cliff has 54 types of ratings, spanning every flight category. He has been a flight dispatcher, parachute rigger, and flight engineer as well as having logged more than 31,000 hours in flight.

Cliff showing his many certifications.

Irene Leverton
March 3, 1927 – July 23, 2017

Irene's mother and her aunt gave her a model airplane kit when she was about six years old.[67] She loved it and built many more models as a child. She would stand on the porch of her third-floor apartment in Chicago and watch her models fly to street level. Her father once bought her a train set, but she couldn't care less about it. She loved airplanes! She didn't like dolls either but dreamed of the day when she could fly an airplane. She was an only child and never married.

Her father was born in Britain and was an ace pilot for the Canadian Army in World War I. He disliked the British because they seemed to move the Americans and Canadians to the front of any battle, causing them to be killed first. Her father was injured in the war and died when she was about nine or ten. Her mother had taught piano, but after the death of her husband, she became a scrubwoman.

Irene was an amazing pioneer in the field of aviation. To say flying was an obsession for her doesn't come close. Many times, she lived out of her car in her pursuits to fly. She began her aviation career in 1949 as an agricultural crop duster, which was rare for a woman. Once she had been crop dusting from Urschel Field for William Rusk and had hit the corn. Ray Miller went to the field to help after her plane flipped upside down. She did this for about four seasons before she quit because she didn't like the new equipment.

Just a portion of Irene's many flight logbooks.

67. Phone conversations on March 14, March 18, and April 2, 2013.

Irene then became a flight instructor and a check pilot. In the 1960s she was selected as a candidate for the Mercury 13 space project, which secretly trained women to become astronauts for America's first human spaceflight. Her flying career spanned 65 years, flying 25 types of multi-engine aircraft plus dozens of single-engine aircraft. She logged 25,768 hours of flight time.

The Smithsonian requested some of her things. She declined as she didn't want to divide her aviation mementos among different museums. For 69 years Irene had been a member of an international organization of women pilots named the Ninety-Nines. She thought her memorabilia would be most fitting for the Ninety-Nines Museum of Women Pilots in Oklahoma City, Oklahoma.

*Irene with her painting of aviation hero
General James Doolittle.*

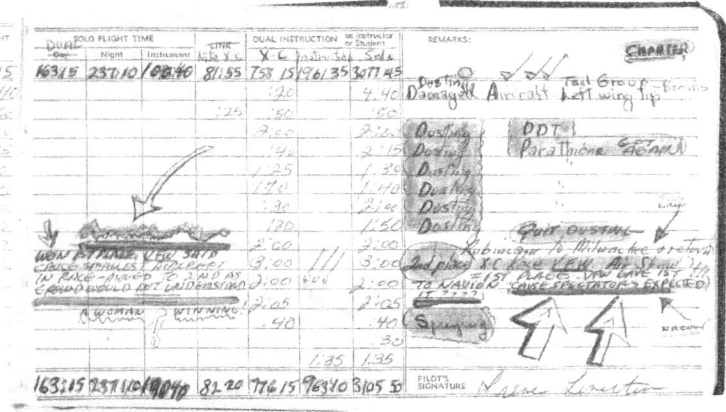

Ray Miller
March 26, 1926–November 10, 2021

Ray pretty much had a photographic memory that made for an enlightened interview. At eighty-seven he still rode his Harley and farmed.[68]

As a young boy he lived with his family on a farm in Wanatah, Indiana. He loved, loved airplanes. His father kiddingly told him he was surprised he didn't ruin more screen doors as every time he heard a plane, he would go flying out the door to watch them.

When he was five years old, he heard the roar of a plane approaching his farm. He raced outside to see a Pitcairn PA-5 Mailwing plane heading his way. He started waving, and the pilot waved and dipped his wing. It was a moment in his life that still gives him great joy when he thinks about it.

The first time he drove a car after getting his license in 1943 or 1944, he headed for Valparaiso, seeking the airport. He finally found the airport and met Claude Lindberg. He wanted to take a plane ride and was excited since he had never been so close to an actual plane. The cost of the ride in that J-5 Cub was $6.

Claude Lindberg asked Ray, "Do you know why an airplane can fly?" Ray had read every issue of *Popular Aviation* and could easily answer all the questions. Claude told him to return to Urschel Field the following Sunday at 10 a.m. for a lesson. Sundays thereafter he took a 30-minute lesson, as flight time was $12 an hour, and he earned only $10 a week from his farm chores. Ray felt an overwhelming joy when he was able to feel the stick come back, moving the plane. They went to 600 feet, made a turn, and then climbed to 800 feet. As they approached the runway and just before landing, he would hit the throttle and take off again. During another lesson Claude handed Ray a parachute, and up they went in a J-3 Cub to 5,000 feet. They did stalls, spins, and snap rolls; Ray loved

---

68. Phone conversations on January 8 and February 3, 2013.

it! The plane had no brakes, and he remembered the number 25 on the side of that plane.

He had ten hours of instruction before he soloed. He did not tell his parents for a long time that he was involved in aviation. After flying solo, the cost was reduced by 50 percent to $6 an hour. Ray thinks Urschel Field had about four Cub trainers at the time.

After he soloed at Urschel Field, he went to Johnson Sports Shop in Valparaiso the same day. He bought a model kit of the same type of Cub that he had soloed in and went home to build it. He later went back to Johnson's to buy some dope to put on the wings and thought it was too expensive. He went to Urschel Field and asked Olie Sundelin if he had any he would sell him. The model had a 4.5-foot wing span. He took the dope that Olie had sold him and put it all over the model. He didn't realize the dope for airplanes was a lot stronger than what they make for models. The dope shrunk the covering and crushed the model plane.

Ray told this story of going to Urschel Field for a lesson way before he soloed: Parked by the office next to the south hangar was a brand-new North American P-51 Mustang. Ray went into the office, but everyone was outside looking at the plane. Ray couldn't believe it since it was supposed to be the greatest plane used in the war. It had a Rolls Royce engine in it. Claude Lindberg wanted to move it because it was in the way of getting the trainer planes out of the hangar. Ray climbed up on the wing, looked into the cockpit, and then stated he wasn't going to touch anything on that plane. Major Chuck Hoover had flown it to the airport, parked it, and spent the night with relatives. The next morning Major Hoover came to the airport with several cars full of people. He was dressed in his uniform. Ray said it was a beautiful sound when the engine came to life. Chuck went to the north end of the runway, and with the engine screaming, the plane went vertical. On takeoff the plane didn't appear to be lifting off, but when Chuck lifted the wheels, it just leaped up and shot straight up. It had a 1500-horsepower engine. He used only half of the runway to do this. He would be gone for a few minutes and then returned roaring along the runway. He did this again, finally waving goodbye as he took off.

Ray thought Olie Sundelin was a very intelligent person and just a wonderful guy. One day *Popular Aviation Magazine* brought a Luscombe to Urschel Field. They would switch the plug wires to make the plane run rough to see if the mechanics at the different fields could detect this. They taxied up to the airport, and Olie came out to see what he could do for them. He figured it out very quickly but was a little upset that they were trying to trick him. They were very impressed with his expertise and did an article on him in their magazine.

Ray had a very close friend named Richard Baske, a very cautious guy, who also took flying lessons. They had soloed on the same day within an hour of each other. Ray had by then confided to his parents that he was taking lessons at the airport. Claude permitted them to fly to their farms. Ray's parents had purchased a larger farm in La Crosse, Indiana, when Ray was twelve, and Richard lived in Hanna, Indiana. They talked and decided that Richard would take off first and make a wide turn, and then Ray would take off and cut across the field. Flying in J-3 Cubs, they were going to meet up at Lincolnway and U.S. Route 30 and fly in formation for a while. They were getting close to their meet-up spot, and Ray was about a half-mile behind Richard. They were flying at about 800 feet. All of a sudden, Richard was going nose down. Ray thought he was going to crash, but Richard was able to pull up just in the nick of time. This was something that they had not practiced. They flew side by side, and then Richard headed for Hanna as Ray turned off and headed for La Crosse. He was thrilled to see both of his parents outside and tipped his wings and waved to them as he headed back to Urschel Field. After they landed, he asked Richard why he had almost killed himself. Richard was very embarrassed. Richard had the door open on the plane, and when he looked back, he could see his tail. He thought it was Ray's wing and that they were way too close and were going to crash, so he took evasive action. He scared himself, and they never talked about it again.

Sometime in the early 1940s, Ray went to the office at Urschel Field. On the bulletin board was an official telegram from the War Department. He couldn't believe what it was requiring, since he had not heard about requisitions. Claude Lindberg told him the telegram had come in the day before.

The telegram read:

> You will have the Staggerwing Beechcraft ready to depart on Monday morning at 8. All the papers concerning the plane should be placed in the cockpit. The Army Air Forces will

125

come to requisition the plane for the duration of hostilities. At the end of the hostilities, you will be sent money for its value based on when we took it.

This was a beautiful single-engine plane made by Pratt & Whitney. It was the fastest airplane at that time, even faster than anything owned by the military. When World War II was over, another telegram arrived at Urschel Field from the War Department stating that the owner could come to Louisville, Kentucky, to pick up that plane, or the government would send money for the value of the plane. As Ray told the story, the owner chose to go to Louisville, not knowing what shape the plane would be in. The government had put in a new engine, Goodyear tires, and the latest radio. The plane was even repainted the way it was originally. The owner was thrilled and couldn't wait to get back to Urschel Field to show everyone.

When Ray was twenty years old, he bought a motorcycle and met a friend who also had a motorcycle at Urschel Field. Everyone was talking about all the planes at the Lansing Airport in Illinois. The two of them took off for Lansing, and when they arrived, they were just amazed at the hundreds of new military planes. They went to the office, where they were given paperwork, and were told to walk around to inspect the various planes. Most of these planes were worth $30,000 and up. The man at the office could not believe they didn't bid on a plane. Later that day they came back to Urschel Field and were surprised at what they saw. There sat Maury Anderson and Carl Harvil's recently purchased PT-1 just like the ones they had seen. Ray figured they had paid about $20,000 but was stunned to find out they had paid only $350, which also included the full tank of gas. The Army had so many planes that the person with the highest bid got the plane no matter what the bid. He realized he could have bid $100 for a P-51. However, at that time, he had no money to purchase anything.

Another interesting story he recalled about Urschel Field was the time in 1947 when an Army training plane landed in a cornfield adjacent to the field. A pilot was doing his first long cross-country solo flight and was lost. His superiors told him to take down the fence and have his plane towed to Urschel Field.

Ray acquired many solo flying hours but did not get his license until 1952 because he had married, bought a farm, and started having children.

In 1952 his brother-in-law Joe McCormick told Ray that if he found a plane, he would buy it and give him half ownership. They were great friends. They went to Urschel Field and found a Luscombe 8-A plane that they liked. They were told the owner wanted $1,500 for it. Joe said that was too much, and he told Ray he would pay $1,200, finally deciding on making a $900 offer. They called the owner and were told the owner was heading to the airport. Joe and Ray assumed it was a man. Up rolled a little red convertible, and a beautiful woman stepped out wearing short shorts and a skimpy top with red hair piled high on her head. She said, "I want $1,500 for my plane." Joe immediately said, "OK! We'll take it!" A very surprised Ray asked Joe why he didn't offer less. He stated that he felt sorry for the woman because she couldn't afford clothes. Ray got the most use of that plane, as Joe did not fly much.

Ray had built a hangar on his farm. He moved his house to higher ground and would move the hangar later. He left his plane outside one night but hadn't tied it down properly. A wind came by that night and destroyed the Luscombe. He sold it for parts through the *Trade-A-Plane* listings, getting enough to purchase another Luscombe, this time with metal wings.

One day Ray was at the airport with his friend Don Holst. They were getting ready to leave the airport and were asked to stay and help with something. A man was coming from Hobart in a J-2 Cub. Ray said this was a cheap airplane, stripped to nothing, two cylinders with a 40-horsepower engine. It was coming to Urschel Field for its 100-hour check-up. Ray and his friend were told to go to the intersection of the two runways and wait for the plane. When it attempted to land, they were to grab it by the struts up by the wings. It was going to be impossible for this man to land the plane. The wind was up, it was a warm day, and the thermals would keep him in the air. Well, here came the J-2 Cub. The pilot bumped the ground and bounced back into the air. Ray and Don grabbed the plane, and while it was still running, with the pilot in the plane, they walked it to the hangar.

Ray was at Urschel Field for the first flight of the Knight Twister, which was on a beautiful Sunday. Ray had never seen a home-built airplane. It was sitting by the south hangar, and a crowd of people were around it. He said the plane took off down the runway and flew off into the distance. As the plane was coming in to land, it came in too fast and barely stopped at the end of the runway. Maury Anderson was sitting in the pilot's seat and was breathing hard, seeming a little scared. He had been flying with the stick as far forward as he could. Ray said a lot of the men discussed what happened and decided to move the engine 7 inches forward.

During the big air show in the early 1950s, Willard Rusk advertised on the bulletin board at the office that he would give anyone $100 if they would parachute out of a plane for the air show. A few days later a very small woman showed up and said she wanted to jump. Willard was thrilled because he thought it would be even more special to have a woman jump. She was an experienced pilot but had never jumped from a plane. She wanted to practice, so they put two parachutes on her and went up to 5,000 feet. The weather was very hot with big thermals. Well, she jumped, pulled the first chute, and started coming down to land at Urschel Field. When she got to about 1,000 feet, she started floating away toward South Bend, Indiana. She decided to pull the second chute and floated higher. A couple of men jumped in a car and started following her. They were yelling for her to shed the second chute. She finally came down at Studebaker Hill in South Bend. She was being dragged, and the men got out to help her. Undeterred, she jumped from a plane the next day at the air show. The weather was perfect, and she made a great jump.

Ray had a friend who was badly crippled. He asked Ray if he would go to Indianapolis, Indiana, with him to visit a friend. They had someone else along to pilot the Stinson plane. They landed at Shanks Airport on the north side of Indy. They stayed hours longer than they had intended and headed home. A beautiful full moon was lighting the sky, and the ground below was covered in snow. When they were approaching Urschel Field, they could see it from very far away, since the snow reflected the moonlight, and Willard Rusk had lighted kerosene pots lined up. Willard was furious with them since they were hours overdue.

Ray remembers that Willard often flew a Beechcraft Bonanza in the 1950s from Urschel Field to Midway Airport. He flew many parts and machines from Urschel Laboratories to Midway to be put on planes heading all over the country. Willard would also take students who were on the GI Bill to Midway with him. This was a great opportunity since they could get training coming into a controlled field.

Another story Ray told was when Ray was leading three brand-new Cessna 150s from Wichita Falls, Kansas, to Urschel Field. One of the pilots radioed Ray that he was out of fuel. Ray asked him if he smelled any gas, and he answered "No." Ray told him to follow him and that they would try to land at the airport in Kankakee, Illinois, where his friend Willard Rusk had moved. He told the other pilots to head to Urschel Field. After the pilot landed safely at Kankakee, Ray landed behind him. Willard Rusk came out of the office with a big smile, thinking he knew what had happened. He asked Ray if the pilot had been flying sideways. The pilot had been flying with his right wing up in order to see Ray. The right tank had emptied into the left tank, leaving the right tank empty. The pilot was somewhat inexperienced and didn't realize he had plenty of fuel. Ray liked and admired Willard, and this was the last time they saw each other.

Ray commented on Mark Murvihill, who was just excellent at all that he did. Mark could rebuild wooden planes better than when they were new. He even rebuilt a Dart plane for one of his friends.

Ray's father, Frank Miller, was really good friends with Siverd Bodin. They both collected farm equipment. One day he went to the Bodin's farm with his father. Siverd had two J-5 Cubs that had been wrecked. One had a crushed tail; the other had a broken nose. Using a hacksaw, he cut the good tail from one plane and was going to put it on the other plane. Frank asked him if he had a license to do that, and Siverd said he would do a better job than anyone he knew.

Siverd and his brother had lights on the runway at their airport. Siverd did not like that they had put lights on the runway after it was done. Often pilots flying overhead would click their microphone transmit button three times to activate the field lights. Some were just stinkers and wanted to see if the lights would come on. The lights were always working and would stay on for 20 minutes. Siverd would wait to see if anyone was landing and would finally realize he was being tricked.

Ray knew a man by the name of Harvey Arnold whose nickname was "Bunny." He lived on Evans Avenue in Valparaiso on a large farm. In the 1950s he owned a J-5 Cub that had glass overhead that allowed you to look straight up and out of the plane. On a beautiful day in March, he decided to fly south to Kokomo, Indiana, or maybe even a little south of there. As he encountered heavy rains and cold temperatures, he decided to land. He called his wife, and she drove down to bring him home. He went back a few days later to get the plane. It was very cold, but the skies were clear. As he was flying, he started getting cold, and he wasn't thinking very well. He was going into hypothermia. He had never been so cold and thought he could be dying. Ahead was Bunker Hill Air Force Base (now Grissom Air Reserve Base), and he knew you never landed at a military base unless it was an extreme emergency. He didn't care if they shot him. He knew he had to land his plane. After he landed the military police surrounded his plane. They got him out and he couldn't stand. They took him to the office and were nasty to him. They realized what the problem was and put him into a very warm shower. They housed his plane in a hangar, where it stayed for a few days. The officers at the base inspected his plane and found that, while his plane was sitting, it had rained, and the water had leaked through the overhead glass and froze. Harvey had been sitting on, essentially, a block of ice. His wife had to come and get him again because they weren't going to release the plane for a few more days until they received the OK from Washington. She was not very happy since she didn't want him flying in the first place.

One last recollection of Ray's was the time Siverd Bodin and he were getting ready to leave South Bend Airport. A Lockheed Constellation was in front of them on the runway. The control tower told Siverd, who was flying a Cessna Skyhawk, to follow the Constellation out. The pilot of the Constellation started energizing the props. This just about tore up the Cessna. Siverd called the pilot and told him he was tearing them up and to pull up a couple of hoe handles. The pilot had never heard this term, and not knowing Siverd was a farmer, it took him a while to figure out what Siverd was saying. He apologized since he didn't know they were behind him.

Bernard (Bernie) Rodgers

April 22, 1929–October 31, 2011

B ernie grew up always wanting to fly.[69] His senior high school teacher told everyone that Bernie was smart enough to be whatever he wanted to become. She couldn't believe that all he wanted to do was fly! After Bernie graduated from high school in 1947, he received his Maintenance Certificate from the Tulsa School of Aeronautics in Oklahoma after one year of study.

At the beginning of the Korean War in 1951, he was drafted into the Army. When he got out of the service, he worked in Plymouth, Indiana, at a private airstrip used by a group of people who had their own aircraft. One of the pilots urged him to get his private pilot's license, which he earned at South Bend Airport. The head of that airport wanted Bernie to take his position since he was retiring; however, Bernie did not accept the offer.

Photo Compliments of:
Bernie Rodgers
1955

Bernie became the head mechanic at Urschel Field in 1955, living in Bud Winder's old house, which was the small house that William Urschel built on the airport property. Many pilots stayed in this house over the years; it had a living room and kitchen as well as two bedrooms; one of the bedrooms had three cots. His wife Rochelle never forgot the

69. Phone conversation with wife Rochelle on December 22, 2012.

time she opened the door and saw a big snake curled up on the chenille bedspread; it scared her, and she wondered how many more were in the house. Rochelle and Bernie lived in that house from September through October 1956, while waiting for their rental house to become available on Flint Lake. The three pilots in the house at that time, including Keith Baird, had to move out while Bernie and Rochelle used it.

She remembers one time when Willard Rusk wanted to promote the airport. For the first time in the history of the airfield, around 1959 or 1960, they used the north hangar for a big dance. The women made a lot of food, musicians were hired, and all had a wonderful time. Social life usually involved playing cards with the whole group, which continued even after everyone switched to Porter County Airport.

After the large north hangar burned down in 1961, Willard decided to move to Kankakee, Illinois. He left Bernie at the airport to clean up the mess and to take inventory of all that was left at the airport, requiring months to complete. Willard wanted him to move to Kankakee with him. Bernie decided he wanted to build a business at Porter County Airport. In 1962 he started Professional Aviation, Inc. He had the business for more than 40 years, selling his interest to his partner Larry Bub when he retired in 1995. Bernie was also an excellent instructor as evidenced by his many awards.

James Slocum

August 24, 1937–

Charles Rusk mentioned his flight instructor, Jim, who he thought lived in or near Atlanta, Georgia. Luckily, I was able to find him in only an hour and talk with him.[70] Yay!

Jim always had a fascination with flying. In 1950 when he was thirteen, he asked his parents if they would take him to Urschel Field, so he could go up in a plane. Willard Rusk took the whole family up in a Stinson Voyager for a 15-to-20-minute ride, totally hooking Jim. Willard offered him a weekend and summer job as a line person. He gassed planes, washed them, and helped put them away at night. He was happy to leave his job on a milk route to work at the airport. He would ride his bike 3 miles to get there. After a while he was able to buy a motor scooter; later he and his sister shared a car.

He helped Bernie Rodgers, an experienced mechanic and Korean War veteran, build a heated, metal maintenance building in front of the south hangar. Large doors allowed planes to be brought inside for work. They overhauled engines and re-covered planes with fabric. The bathroom was in the south hangar.

Jim offered interesting information on using planes for spraying. Willard Rusk would spray the fairgrounds for mosquitos in a special Luscombe plane equipped for spraying. Later crop dusters used a PA-18A, which is the agricultural version of the Super Cub, incorporating a slightly different rear-fuselage profile to allow the spray tank to fit in the rear-seat position. Wire cutters were placed in front of the landing gear which could cut telephone wires if needed. A wire ran from the top of the rudder to the top of the fuselage. If you flew under a wire, it would deflect the wire from tearing off the rudder. Sometimes Willard Rusk would bring a truck with the chemicals, so the plane would not have to fly back to the airport.

At Urschel Field around 1 p.m. on August 18, 1952, Jim gassed up a Vultee BT-13, which was a World War II trainer with a fixed gear. That plane was big, heavy, and slow. The secondary control was replaced with a bench seat, so that two passengers could ride tandem in the back of the plane. Mr. Wait, a steel-mill employee, permitted Joe Cook to fly his

70. Conversations with Jim on December 1, 2012, March 5, 2013, and May 9, 2013.

133

plane. Joe worked at the airport doing all kinds of things such as dusting/spraying and instructing. He had been a pilot during the war and was very familiar with the BT-13. Joe had been in a car accident earlier that summer, still had many bandages, and had not totally recovered from that accident. Joe asked Jim if he wanted to go up with him. Jim declined, so Joe took up Benny Ripley and Wendell Stoner. Joe made a pass over Urschel Field and came around again really fast. Jim was watching and couldn't understand why Joe was holding the nose up for way too long. It is suspected that Joe had passed out from doing maneuvers. Lacking a secondary back control, the passengers were unable to save themselves. The plane stalled and spun. At about 300 feet the rotation stopped, and the plane went straight into the ground. All were killed on the Serial Warren farm, 5 miles northwest of Valparaiso.[71]

Jim also remembers when Ray Johnson crashed with his children on board. Jim and another person drove there to bring the pieces of the plane back to Urschel Field on a truck that Willard Rusk owned. He said that Ray's Tri-Pacer had started picking up ice, and he had decided to try landing at Terre Haute, Indiana. He started the turn; the plane stalled and went nose-first into the ground. Ray perished, but his three children survived. Jim stated that he couldn't believe anyone survived the crash.

Ray with son Roy and Tri-Pacer 1956

These crashes did not deter Jim's interest in flying. Riding with several pilots just fueled his desire to fly, and at age sixteen, he started flying lessons.

Jim soloed on August 25, 1953, in a Piper A-11. He did a lot of solo flying.

At age seventeen, he thinks, he had his pilot's license when he purchased his first plane in Crown Point, Indiana. Willard Rusk financed his 65-horsepower Aeronca Chief, costing $350. Jim was earning only about 50 to 75 cents an hour but eventually paid off the loan. Willard was his pilot-license instructor. The regulations at the time said that, once

71. "Plane Crashes Northwest of Valparaiso, Three Area Men Killed," *Vidette-Messenger*, August 18, 1952.

someone of Jim's age obtained his license, the pilot could fly family and friends but could not earn any income from flying.

Jim did his cross-country for his pilot's license on July 6, 1954. When he landed at Urschel Field, Irene Leverton, a woman pilot and crop duster, signed his logbook with her certified flight instructor #119509. The men were amazed that a woman did that type of work. Jim flew with her several times. Irene would go on to accrue many accolades in her 65-year aviation career.

Jim traded his Aeronca for a Piper J-3 Cub. He felt it was an even trade. In the Piper J-3 Cub, the pilot sat in the back seat, making it a better trainer, which was important as he was working toward his commercial license, which he earned at age eighteen. The closest FAA inspector was at the towered South Bend Airport. Urschel Field did not have an inspector or a designated pilot examiner. The closest designated pilot examiner was at Cole Airport in Hobart, Indiana, where oral exams and checkrides were held. He and many of the pilots at Urschel Field obtained their licenses at Cole Airport.

While Jim was still eighteen, he started working on his flight instructor's license. Once completed, he did a lot of instructing to earn money and airtime while also dusting and spraying fields. During this time he rented a room from Charles Rusk.

In my conversation with James Deck, James fondly recalled that Jim Slocum gave him and his friends rides in a Piper J-3 Cub.[72] They would take turns; rides were $1 each way, which would pay for the gas. The Piper had one door, and you could open the top or the bottom. They would open part of the door. Whenever they went up, Jim Slocum would give them two choices: Choice 1 was to fly very low over the Dunes and wave to all the girls. Choice 2 was to fly out to Sager Lake and buzz the nudist colony. They never saw anything, but their buddies at high school did not know this.

In 1957 he married and moved to Sarasota, Florida, because he was able to work full time as a flight instructor even in the winters when Urschel Field was not as busy due to its weather. He read about the job in the *Trade-A-Plane* tabloid. He stayed there for about 3 or 4 months before moving to a more lucrative GI Bill-approved flight program in St.

---

72. Phone conversation with James Deck on January 8, 2013.

Petersburg, Florida. He was earning good money as a flight instructor, but more importantly, he was building hours in the air.

In 1959 Jim again saw a *Trade-A-Plane* ad for a civilian contract instructor at the Fort Rucker Army Base in Alabama. At the beginning of their training, the student pilots received about 120 hours of training in an L-19 Cessna.

Brothers Loren and Eldon Peters from Rensselaer, Indiana, worked at Urschel Field, crop dusting for Willard Rusk. Eldon was also a wingwalker in the Cole Brothers Air Show. Loren was a pilot for Indianapolis-based Lake Central Airlines. After several mergers the company became part of US Airways. Loren called Jim to tell him they were looking for pilots. Jim was hired in 1961 to co-pilot in a DC-3. When business was slow, pilots were furloughed. Jim would find temporary flying jobs in between, but by the third furlough he quit and flew full time for Eastern Airlines.

Jim recalled other pilots he knew who flew for major airlines:

Jim Slocum	Eastern	Carroll Dietz	Eastern
Bill Stevens	Eastern	Larry Trapp	US Airways
Eldon Peters	US Airways	Loren Peters	US Airways

Toward the end of our conversation, he talked about his memories of Urschel Field, specifically mentioning the air shows when a Cub would land on a special trailer pulled by a car going about 50 miles per hour down the field. The hill northeast of the north hangar that led to Mark Mulvihill's business was the site many people would use for weekend picnics because it was a perfect spot to watch planes as they took off or landed. Kids of all ages were welcome to hang around the airport. He said the airport had a really fun and welcoming feeling for all the pilots and their families. Everyone talked the same language, and there were always many planes and lots of pilots out there flying them. Jim believes that Urschel Field was a benchmark for what a small airport should be like.

John McGuire

April 14, 1926–December 29, 2017

As a child living in Chicago, John loved airplanes. He built model planes along with some of the neighborhood boys when he was young.[73]

John wanted to join the Army Air Forces during World War II, but his acuity wasn't good enough. He ended up serving in the U.S. Army Coast Artillery Corps with an anti-aircraft unit in the Philippines.

He often passed the Chicago-Hammond Airport on his way to work as an electrical mechanical engineer. One day he turned in and asked what it took to become a pilot. He quickly made arrangements to start taking lessons. After five hours of instruction in a Piper J-3 Cub, he soloed. He was also checked out in a Taylorcraft airplane. His instructors wanted him to become acquainted with all kinds of aircraft. When asked when he became hooked on flying, he explained that he was hooked way before his first plane ride. He felt very comfortable in a plane as he understood flight, knew what a rudder was, what the stick did, and everything about the plane.

His job required him to cover three different states: Michigan, Indiana, and Illinois. He searched to find a town that would make his job accessible to all parts of his territory. He decided that Valparaiso seemed like a great place to live. After moving to Valparaiso in 1954, he explored the facilities at Urschel Field to continue his lessons.

Initially, he did not tell his wife that he was flying. Then one day he asked his wife to come out to Urschel Field with him. She thought they might be taking a ride in a plane. Before she knew it, John was in a plane going down the runway and taking off. She knew this was a love of his, so she did not discourage him from going forward and getting his license. Since his job territory included Illinois, he took his first cross-country flight out of Joliet. His second cross-country took him to Cedar Rapids, Iowa. Cross-country jaunts were a requirement for earning his pilot's license. He flew a Cessna 140 to do this.

One of his favorite planes at Urschel Field was the Navion. John would rent it from Willard Rusk. The plane seated four and had a 185-horsepower Continental engine. The number on that plane was N8885H. It was originally made for the civilian market but was also used in World

---

73. Conversation with John McGuire on January 7, 2013.

War II. Another favorite was the Cessna 195, which was a World War II instrument trainer with a 245-horsepower Jacobs engine. His least favorite plane was the J-3 Cub because you had to solo from the back seat.

John never went for a multiple-engine license. When flying for work, he flew to both coasts with an ATR pilot in a Merlin IIIB. John flew in the right seat, and the pilot let him fly the plane except for takeoffs and landings.

John liked Willard Rusk. Willard would allow the private pilots to fly people to Midway Airport. Willard did not pay these pilots but would give them airtime. Willard did not want to hire commercial pilots to do this since he would have to pay them. John did not mind because he loved to fly. The passengers were usually flown in a Tri-Pacer. This plane had a luggage compartment that could hold two large suitcases. When John landed, he would talk to ground control and tell them how many passengers he had on board. He was directed to the Eastern or American terminal and would taxi right up next to the jets. Employees would come out to greet them, guide them inside, and then escort them onto their next plane. John had logged in his book that two of these flights took place on May 12, 1960, and May 26, 1960. He made other trips after this. He stated that Midway at that time was the busiest airport in the world.

John did get his instrument rating in early 1960. He trained in the C-3 Link Trainer in the north hangar. He said it was a really old relic used to train pilots in World War II, but Willard was glad to have it. Bob Baird was his instructor for the trainer.

He was sad when Urschel Field closed in 1963, as he loved going out there. John reminisced in this email, sent on January 7, 2013:

> In reviewing a very old pilot logbook, I found my first flight time at Urschel Field was May 13, 1954, where I was checked out in an Aeronca Champ 84157, under the guidance of Russ Merrihew. Though I spent time with several different instructors there, including Willard Rusk, Merrihew became my primary instructor while striving for my private pilot's license. He later left to fly for a growing freight airline, Flying Tiger Airlines. Another of my instructors, Carroll Dietz, went on to fly for Eastern Airlines.

On June 5, 1956, Russ Merrihew rode over to the South Bend Airport, where I was to take my private-license flight examination with Lester Cooling, then representing the CAA, the forerunner of the present FAA. On the strength of my flight performance, Merrihew was to receive an Examiners rating, and I earned my private pilot's license. Fortunately, on that day I performed up to the expectations of Mr. Cooling.

From that time on I checked out and used several different aircraft from Urschel Field. These planes ranged from Piper Tri-Pacers (club members could rent them at $7 an hour with fuel) to Bonanzas and 195 Cessnas. The last record I have of activity at Urschel Field is April 9, 1962. The picture is a photo of my son Jack with a V-77 Stinson.

V-77 STINSON   URSCHEL FIELD   JACK McGUIRE

Relating some tales of Urschel Field, I will pass on one of the more renowned of the well-known tales. This deals with the hill at the north end of the sod runway. This dilemma was not, ordinarily, apparent to a pilot not familiar with this field. The runway sloped down from north to south causing an approaching aircraft to continue to float above the descending ground until the aircraft impacted the level segment of the runway. This almost always caused less than the perfect landing the pilot was anticipating.

John Kane
January 21, 1919–April 15, 1972

John was an Army veteran of World War II, serving in the National Guard for 20 years, and was part of the Civil Air Patrol.[74] He moved to Valparaiso to help his brother Charles run his riding stables. In 1948 John joined the Valparaiso Police Department.

John received his pilot's license using the GI Bill at Urschel Field. He flew many times with Willard Rusk in a Tri-Pacer and practiced with a Piper Cub for his license.

One time while flying his family to Dayton, Ohio, he approached the field too fast, scaring everyone, but thankfully, he was able to land. All the pilots who were at the airport rushed to the plane to see if everyone was OK.

His son Art has never forgotten when his father took him up in a Tri-Pacer when he was five years old and saw from on high all the trains and green fields.

John quit flying when it became too expensive.

---

74. Phone conversation on May 15, 2015, with John's son Art.

Lloyd Kissinger

March 6, 1933–

Lloyd's ideas of flying began when he was five years old as he joined his family at a farm field.[75] A wheatfield on the south side of Crocker had some stubble in it. People were asked to walk on the field to stomp the stubble down. In came a Piper Cub flown by Bus Babcock. Everyone was thrilled. He remembers the plane flew rather slowly, and he thinks it had a 38-horsepower engine in it. When Bus took off, he flew it *under* the power lines. The wing struts were 2 x 4s. He was not allowed to take a ride in the plane, but his older brothers were able to fly that day.

Lloyd started at age eight building every type of World War II model plane after his three older brothers went to war. He kept a scrapbook of all the fighter planes and of any plane he saw in the newspaper. His mother hated the war and was under so much stress with her boys in the service that one day his mother just threw the whole scrapbook away. He wished he still had it.

When Lloyd was sixteen, he had the urge to learn to fly. He wanted to go to Urschel Field to take flying lessons but chose to save for college instead. In 1952 when Lloyd was nineteen years old, he went to West Virginia to see a girl he knew. One of her girlfriends had a father who owned the airport. This man took Lloyd flying in a Tri-Pacer and let him fly it. They flew at 1,000 feet over the Ohio River. When they were coming in, he let Lloyd land the plane. Lloyd was hooked.

Shortly after that, he was drafted. A major told him he could fly the L-19 plane, but he would have to stay in for four years, or two years longer than he originally planned. After basic training he was offered an appointment to West Point by this same major and another person. He also declined those offers. Looking back, he regrets that he didn't take the appointment. He would have had to stay no more than a total of

75. Conversation on June 18, 2018.

eight years. He said it would have opened many doors for him if he had gone to the academy.

Lloyd married in June 1955 and lived in Porter, Indiana. Shortly thereafter he decided to use the GI Bill to learn to fly. He flew with Steve Kreshock a few times to make sure that this was how he wanted to use the GI Bill. Keith Baird and Steve Kreshock taught him at Urschel Field. Using the Aeronca Champ N2552E and the Tri-Pacer N82777, he practiced his flying. He soloed on October 2, 1957. He loved that day and was yelling "Whoopie" as he flew.

When he was twenty-six, he was out flying and flew across the state line to Chatsworth, Illinois. That airport had a long runway. He decided he didn't need to use the whole runway when he took off and barely cleared some buildings. He decided that when instructed to always use the whole runway, he had better take heed!

He flew a lot with his friend Warren Trowbridge. They used to go out and fly side by side. Willard Rusk gave them all kinds of heck and told them not to do it again. Lloyd flew many times without his private pilot's license, taking up many passengers. He decided that he should probably get his license; Claude Lindberg, who was a CAA designated examiner, told him to go to the Gary Airport and get his checkride. He got it on July 15, 1961, from Denny Cole at the Sky Ranch Airport. Denny Cole was a cousin to Duane Cole of the famous Cole Brothers.

His favorite planes to fly were the 90-horsepower Champ and the Piper PA-12. He liked the PA-12 since he thought it was a comfortable plane to fly and handled well. His least favorite plane was an L-4 Stinson, a very heavy two-place World War II artillery plane. Mark Murvihill owned this plane and told Lloyd to come in closer to the runway when landing it because he was having thumper landings. He recalled Urschel Field was a very busy place, and the sky always seemed full of planes. The last time Lloyd flew was in 2003.

Betty Kuehl-Heffner

March 23, 1941–February 4, 2024

Betty in 1958 by Aeronca Champion NC2552E

Betty's house is located on the north side of Bullseye Lake in Valparaiso. The house was built almost 173 years ago, in about 1850. Betty was the fourth generation to reside in the house, which is just north of where Urschel Field was located. Her mom and dad moved into the house in the spring of 1947. They farmed 40 acres, rotating various crops over the years.[76]

Betty always loved seeing all the planes go over her house. One day she was sitting in a rowboat on Bullseye Lake, watching plane after plane fly overhead. Something came over her that day, and she decided she had to learn to fly a plane. Her parents were totally against her flying and thought it was just too dangerous. In 1955 she started going to the airport just to hang out.

Betty's first airport story was about Raymond Johnson, who lived close to the Kuehls and owned a Piper Tri-Pacer. He had three children whom he would take flying. Finally, Betty's father told her she could go up with Raymond. The three children sat in the back. They flew to Whiting, Indiana, where there was a huge fire raging at a refinery. Betty was about fourteen years old at the time and just loved going on that plane ride.

Raymond was killed in 1957, coming back from Florida. He had three of his four children with him. Betty said that Paul Black, another pilot, was flying his plane from Florida, and all the planes set down in Atlanta. Paul decided to stay put and told Ray not to head home since the weather north was getting scary. Raymond decided to press on and crashed in Terre Haute, Indiana, while attempting to land in a severe thunderstorm. All three of his children survived; unfortunately, he did not.

---

76. Conversations on November 30, 2012, December 12, 2012, May 4, 2013, and May 6, 2023.

In 1957 when Betty was sixteen years old, she started working at the airport. She wanted to earn enough money to take lessons, and her first job was washing airplanes for other pilots. She finally worked her way up to assisting in the office, where she oversaw a lot of the GI Bill paperwork.

Betty vividly recalled her flight training and details about Urschel Field's two runways: the north/south, which was the longest, and the east/west runway. Pilots and students were required to taxi the distance of the N/S runway to the north end to take off into the south winds. Everyone was required to hug the west side of the runway, keeping an open area with enough space for planes to land. If you were in a plane with tricycle gear, such as a Tri-Pacer, there is no problem seeing through the windshield to see what is in front of the airplane. However, if you are in a tail dragger, such as an Aeronca Champion, the nose of the plane rides high and obstructs your forward view. While taxiing in a tail dragger, to see what is ahead of the plane, you must gently zigzag the plane forward. This allows you to look out of a side window with each zig or zag to see what is in front of the plane.

Taxiing up to the north end of the N/S runway, Betty was in the front seat of the Aeronca Champion with her instructor, Keith Baird, in the rear seat; Baird was doing the zig-zag routine. Almost at the north end of the runway, Keith slammed on the brakes, stopping the plane instantly. Betty looked back at Keith and asked him why he'd stopped the plane. He told her to take a look out the window. There, crossing the runway, was the reason—in black and white. A family of five skunks were crossing the runway directly in front of the plane. Betty learned to look more carefully from then on.

A student pilot must solo on a cross-country flight with a distance of 100 miles on one of three legs before taking the test flight for a private pilot's license. Betty recalled her cross-country originating at Urschel Field. The first leg was from Valparaiso to Fort Wayne, Indiana; the second leg was from Fort Wayne to Goshen, Indiana; the third leg was from Goshen back to Urschel Field. Betty made the flight from Valparaiso to Fort Wayne without any problem. The day was perfect for flying. Betty set down in Fort Wayne, refueled, and prepared for takeoff to Goshen. Again having a trouble-free, perfect flight, she arrived at Goshen. After refueling, she left Goshen en route back to Valparaiso.

She was approximately 12 miles out from Urschel Field when she became aware that the airplane's motor was losing RPMs (revolutions per minute made by the propeller). No matter what she tried, even at full throttle, the RPMs kept dropping. She knew she had a decision to make. Should she set the plane down in a field while she still had a choice, or should she try to make it back to Urschel Field? Betty was confident she could safely make a dead-stick emergency landing if that situation should develop. She managed to limp back to the airport; however, the standard protocol of the proper way to re-enter the flight pattern went out the window.

She made a beeline for the airport, did a sharp right turn, and set the plane down safely on the runway. During this maneuver she cut off another student pilot on his final approach. He was some distance back, and Betty knew there was no possible way that either one was in any danger of a mid-air collision. He had no choice and did a go-around. Betty taxied the plane back to the office building, parked it, and went inside. Entering the building, she realized Baird was pretty hot, but he quickly calmed down after finding out why it happened. Although Betty told Keith about the RPM problem, Keith chalked it up to a case of long cross-country jitters. Betty would have no part of that.

Within ten minutes Betty and Keith were in a takeoff run in the plane. Of course, the takeoff was perfect, and no power problem presented itself. That lasted about five minutes, at which time the RPMs started dropping again. After an expedited landing Keith told the maintenance shop manager, Bernie Rodgers, about the problem. The next day Betty went into the maintenance shop and saw the plane, minus its motor, which lay in many pieces on a large table. Bernie said—and she quotes—"Betty, I don't want to scare you, but I cannot figure out what kept that motor going. It is completely shot!"

Betty believed flight instructors were dedicated people, whose job it was to transfer their knowledge and skills to a novice student. A student's job was to learn what the instructor passed on to them through intense training during endless practices.

If there were commandments for flying, Betty claimed that "Always respect your plane" would be number one. All the instructors constantly reminded their students that if you don't, it could kill you. A good example of that caveat was a pilot named Joe. He owned his own plane, and it was not uncommon for him to push his airplane to the limits, as he was a daredevil. He particularly got a kick out of flying into towering thunderhead clouds. One day Joe flew his plane directly into a severe thunderhead cloud. He went into the cloud in one piece, and the cloud spit him and his plane out in several pieces. He had no respect for himself or his plane.

One day Keith Baird took Betty up flying on a routine training flight, when all of a sudden, Keith pulled the throttle back. He told Betty the plane had just lost its engine, and he wanted to know what she was going to do. This was Betty's first lesson in making an emergency landing. Keith told her she had complete control of the airplane, except for the throttle. Betty quickly scanned the ground down below, looking for a suitable field to put the plane down. She spotted the perfect field, but it was some distance away. Nonetheless, that was her chosen field, and Keith never said a word; he just motioned for her to proceed. As Betty started her glide toward the field, she soon realized they were going to fall short of it. She needed more airspeed, so she slightly lowered the plane's nose just enough to gain a little more airspeed. Then she brought the plane level to stretch the glide. She did this maneuver several times, and it worked. She made it to the field she had chosen. She was now ready to set the plane down.

At about 30 feet from landing, Keith told her she had full throttle control back, and she quickly throttled and regained her flying speed, climbing back to 3,000 feet. Keith told her he didn't think she would have ever made it and congratulated her on doing so. He told her that in any situation requiring an emergency landing, the first place you should look is directly below you. See what is available there before looking elsewhere.

During her training Keith taught her the art of slow flight, which requires throttling back while flying into a headwind. The objective is to fly the plane forward while the headwind pushes against the forward motion resulting in a minimum forward distance gained. During this maneuver a safe flying speed must be maintained to prevent the plane from stalling out. Betty had endlessly practiced this maneuver. She decided to show Keith how well she had mastered this.

Heading into a strong headwind blowing from the south, Betty selected a spot where there were two sets of railroad tracks parallel to each other. As she was approaching the tracks from the north, she began to slowly throttle back. She kept reducing her forward thrust until the airplane was barely moving forward. As the landing gear passed the northernmost rail, she began timing the flight. It took almost ten minutes until the landing gear finally passed over the southernmost rail. After finally getting past the track, she throttled up and returned to the airport, convincing Keith she could do the maneuver.

Urschel Field hosted several flying clubs: Tri-Pacers, Blue Birds, Skyways, Sportsmen, and Flying Aces. Betty was a member of the Flying Aces club, which consisted of Bob Merritt, Bill Stevens, Fred Spafford, Wally Lawrence, Tom Lasco, Max Gray, Bill Doefner, Phil Saxton, William Hesselgrave, Roger Hefferth, Don Beken, and Betty—notably, the only woman. One club rule was no drinking, not ever. You would be bounced out of the club if caught. The fees for the club were $10 a month to help purchase the plane. They leased from Willard Rusk of Rusk Aviation. The Flying Aces' Aeronca Champion airplane was something they were proud of, as it had carpeting and a chrome-plated joystick with white handlebar grips. The instrument panel was fitted with real leather, and they had seat covers made for both seats. The airplane was their baby and was an excellent flying plane, except it had a boo-boo.

One day an FAA flight inspector had come from South Bend to Urschel Field to administer the private pilot's flight test to five students. One of the students was a member of the Flying Aces and was going to be tested in the Flying Aces' Aeronca Champion. During the required pre-flight examination of the plane, the inspector noticed a wrinkle in the plane's fabric on the left side of the fuselage, near the tail section. None of them could explain the wrinkle. The FAA inspector immediately grounded the plane and ordered a piece of fabric to be cut away in the area of the wrinkle. They were all stunned at what was causing the wrinkle—the metal airframe on that side was broken. This could have been a very dangerous situation for all the club members who had flown that plane on many occasions. If it had broken further, the tail could have fallen off the airplane. When the part was being welded, the fabric caught on fire and was quickly extinguished. A member of the club took his flight test in a different Aeronca Champion that day and received his pilot's license.

July 23, 1959, finally came for the private pilot's flight test. It was a Saturday, and five students were scheduled to take the test, Betty being the only woman. The weather that day was not good with a low ceiling and on-again, off-again rain showers. The students, flight instructors, and the FAA test inspector were all gathered inside the office, discussing the weather. Deciding to go ahead with the tests, the inspector yelled, "Ladies first." Betty and the inspector climbed aboard the Piper Tri-Pacer that was used for the radio portion of the test because the Aeronca Champion plane was not equipped with two-way radios. The radio portion of the test, both on the ground and in the air, went fine.

The inspector asked Betty to perform many maneuvers that she learned in her training such as turns, slow-flight turns around pylons, emergency landings, etc. While doing stalls, the nose of the plane started entering the cloud deck. The inspector suggested they return to the airport, as the weather was worsening. Urschel Field had sod runways, and on rainy days any indentation in the ground surface could cause puddles. As Betty brought the plane in for a landing, she kept backward pressure on the yoke; the plane slowed rapidly, with the stall warning blaring. Unfortunately, as the plane touched down, the right main landing gear hit a shallow puddle, causing dirty water to splash upward through the open vent of the aircraft, soaking the pant leg of the inspector. At the exact moment the right wheel hit that puddle, the inspector exclaimed, "Don't hit that puddle!" Betty told him he'd spoken too late. Betty taxied up to the office, parked the plane, and turned off the ignition. The inspector entered the office as Betty waited in the plane.

Betty's treasured model of her Aeronca.

As she was waiting for her inspector, she was contemplating her yet-to-be-done Aeronca Champion flight check. She loved her plane, NC2552E, a 1947 Aeronca Champion, known as the Champ. (Years later when visiting the Neil Armstrong Museum, Betty was amazed to see that Neil had learned to fly in a plane identical to her Aeronca Champion.)

Finally, she entered the office, where the inspector was talking with her instructor Keith telling him he had not intended to give Betty the entire test in that Tri-Pacer but just wanted to know if she could do all the maneuvers. The inspector told Keith that she had performed all of them up to and beyond his expectations, and she was a great pilot. He also said that Betty was better than a lot of male students he had tested. He sat down and wrote out Betty's license. She was the only one to get a license that day because of the weather. Betty was elated and thought this day was the pinnacle day of her entire life.

A couple of days later she found out that when she was up with the inspector, Keith was pacing across the office floor like some nervous expectant father. She thought silently to herself that Keith had nothing to worry about. On August 2, 1959, the *Gary Post* ran a big article with a picture of Betty reporting on her wonderful accomplishment. After she got her pilot's license, her father flew with her on three or four occasions, but her mother, terrified of flying, never did.

Most of the people were successful in getting their pilot's license; however, there is always the exception. One day a student came in and stated he had washed out of several flight schools. Every instructor at Urschel Field gave this man lessons. He had more than 200 hours of dual flying time. They tried everything they could to help him, but he finally washed out at Urschel Field. He did OK at taking off but was terrified to land. It was a really sad day for him when he realized he would never get his license.

Some who had a license may have not deserved one as evidenced by the following story. A pilot came in to land at the south end of the runway. He didn't land into the wind, which all pilots were instructed to do. Betty noticed that the plane had stopped in the middle of the runway. The pilot was trying to turn the plane toward the hangars. Betty noticed the strong south wind was raising the tail of the plane. She yelled to the guys for help, and they all rushed from the office. They didn't quite make it, and the tail went over the top of the plane, nice and easy but ruining the vertical stabilizer.

Tony Skvarek was one of the many students taking flying lessons at Urschel Field. One day Tony was southwest of the airport doing what all students had to do: practice—over and over—maneuvers that he had been taught. Without warning, a thick fog settled in, and Tony was unable to see anything outside of the windows. Knowing it was not safe to fly in the fog and having no instrument training, Tony knew he had to get the plane down. In training for a forced-landing situation, students are taught the first place to look is straight down. In Tony's case he had no other choice, as all he could see was straight down. As luck would have it, the field below was good for a landing. Tony put the plane into a tight circle and spiraled down to an altitude where he figured he could bring the plane in for a safe landing, and that he did. Neither he nor the plane sustained any damage. Tony parked the plane and walked up to a farmhouse. He explained to the people who he was and what had happened. He was able to call the airport, and they sent a car to bring him back to the airport.

The next day a crew went out to fly the plane back to Urschel Field. Be advised: one can get a plane into a small space, but it may not be possible to fly it out of that space. Keith Baird was a top-notch short-field takeoff pilot, but after several failed takeoff attempts, he said it was hopeless to try to fly the plane out of the field. They had to bring in a trailer from the airport, remove the plane's wings, and load everything up onto the trailer to transport the plane back to Urschel Field. Tony read this whole experience as a warning message from above and decided to quit flying. The other pilots respected his decision; all said their goodbyes and never heard from him again.

During the time Betty was flying from Urschel Field, the runway had lights. They were usually turned off at night unless someone requested they stay on so they could land. Urschel Field did not have a restaurant but had a variety of sandwiches in the refrigerator which

Betty's daughter Christy age 4

could be heated in the infrared machine. They also had potato chips and other snacks, an always-full coffee pot, and a soft-drink machine. Betty even told the story of a lady in her sixties with three family members who landed at Urschel Field en route from Pittsburgh, Pennsylvania, to Lincoln, Nebraska, just to get something to eat.

In 1957 the office at Urschel Field was broken into through a window. Betty said a man had been coming day after day to play the pinball machine for hours at a time. During the burglary a file cabinet was broken into, and the pinball machine was torn to pieces. Everyone at Urschel Field had to go to the police station and get fingerprinted. The robbery was traced back to this man who had been there playing the pinball machine.

In the *Prairie Farmer Magazine* Stroller section early in the 1950s, an article claimed that Urschel Field was the busiest privately owned airfield in the United States. Rusk Aviation provided many aviation services from Urschel Field. They crop dusted, taught students, chartered trips, sold airplanes, and offered ambulance flights. In addition, they did frost patrol. Pilots would fly very low over the farm fields to keep the air stirred up, so the crops wouldn't freeze, often buzzing the fields most of the night.

Steve Kreshock, Keith Baird, and Charlie Younce (son of William, who was a member of the first Aero Club at Urschel Field in the 1930s) headed out one cold night. About three in the morning Steve broke out and headed for the airport to refuel. Keith saw him and broke out, deciding to follow Steve. Charlie did the same and thought he was following Keith. Charlie didn't show up at the airport, and that worried Keith and Steve. About 30 minutes later, they saw Charlie coming in to land. Charlie was following what he thought was Keith's taillight but didn't see him turn off. After what seemed like a very long time, he realized he was looking at the planet Venus and turned back toward home.

All the men who did crop dusting wore flight helmets, as it was a very dangerous occupation. Sometime in the late 1940s, Keith Baird's wife Mary saw him crash. She was eight months pregnant and was standing by the hangar when she saw the accident. The men went to the crash site. Keith's helmet was cracked all over like an eggshell, but it did save his life.

Besides all those previously mentioned services operating out of Urschel Field, Betty added two more that Keith Baird offered in his Tri-Pacer. Keith would transport deceased people to their final destinations around the Midwest. The corpse was placed on a stretcher and covered. The stretcher was placed over the top of the front passenger seat reaching from the dash into the back. He told Betty it wasn't unusual for a moan or body twitches to occur. One time a body sat straight up and startled him.

Keith was also on retainer for a wealthy family, whom he would fly every year to the Indianapolis 500. A limo would always pick them up, and Keith was treated to the race and all the activities for the day. He loved that job!

Betty's strangest aviation memory occurred on a beautiful summer Saturday; the sky was clear and blue without a cloud to be found. Betty was busy working at her desk in the office at the field when she took a moment to rest her eyes. As she glanced out a west window, she saw something in the west sky at about a 45-degree angle up from the horizon. The thing was oval, sort of like a giant turkey platter. The edge was razor sharp around the object. The color was all the colors of the rainbow arranged in a swirled mosaic pattern. Betty quickly had everyone at the airport observing the phenomenon; no one had ever seen anything like it. They all watched it for a long time as it remained stationary, and the colors never changed. Of course, no one had a camera. A thick cloud bank was rising from the western horizon. The cloud bank took a long time to reach the edge of this thing before obscuring their vision. The men decided that the thing was nothing more than a massive collection of water droplets. Betty had never seen anything like it previously or since. Was it a natural phenomenon or something else?

It is a fact of life: people can get air sickness, even pilots. It is always a good idea to carry a barf bag. One beautiful flying day, two of Betty's club members were flying in the Aeronca Champion. They set down at an airport and enjoyed a treat of blueberry pie and coffee. On the way back to Urschel Field, the guy in the rear seat got sick, so he slid the window open and stuck his head outside to barf. Big mistake! As he stuck his head out of the window, the propeller blast hit him in the back of the head, causing a minor vortex on his face as he upchucked; the vomit twisted around his face. The pilot did not have any sick sacks on board. What a mess! His flying buddy nearly laughed himself to death. After they landed, both the sick passenger and the plane got a good cleaning. Lesson learned to always have sick sacks on board.

The Vidette-Messenger newspaper on February 28, 1961, ran an article and pictures about the north hangar at Urschel Field burning to the ground. Willard Rusk afterward moved most of his operation to Kankakee, Illinois. Betty followed Willard Rusk to Kankakee to work for him in 1963. She did most of her flying out of Midway Airport starting in 1964. Midway operations were kept active by civilian aviation after all commercial operations had moved to O'Hare Airport.

This final story from Betty occurred at Greater Kankakee Airport, where she relocated with Willard Rusk after Urschel Field closed. One of Rusk's students, named Fred, had recently received his pilot's license, and he decided to take his friend up in a newer Aeronca Champion airplane with tandem seats. They were both big men, sort of like lumberjacks.

With both men in the front seat, most of the plane's weight was in the nose area. During the joyride Fred decided to take the plane up to its ceiling of close to 11,000 feet; while he was up there, the plane went into a spin. As it came down into a tight spin, Fred was unable to pull the plane out of the spin, and it slammed into the ground, killing them both. Unfortunately, only the night before Fred had become engaged to be married. As Betty's instructors told her, and Betty passed on to her colleagues, "Always respect your airplane."

Some major points in a letter dated December 16, 2021, to Cinda Urschel, Betty stated:

- I think a lot about Urschel Field and my time there. Urschel Field was my personal Magic Kingdom, and that kingdom extended far up into the sky.
- Urschel Field was a happy place to be. The people there were always ready to give you a quick smile along with a pleasant greeting. I am not talking only about the employees but also the numerous students who were there learning to fly using the GI Bill, and even the strangers who landed to fuel up and have a bite to eat before continuing on their journey.
- It was as if Urschel Field was surrounded by a gigantic welcome mat. It was a place filled with home hospitality. The old wooden buildings along with the sod runways screamed out, *Welcome, Friends."*

+ I also spent time at several other airports after Urschel Field closed, but those airports could not hold a candle to the feelings Urschel Field emitted; it was unique.

During our visits Betty graciously shared not only her stories but also her many extremely well-organized photo albums. Seeing pictures of so many of these early aviators made these stories come to life. Not only was she a talented pilot, but her memory concerning major and minor events at Urschel was remarkable. We and future generations can thank her for all that she has done in living an honorable life in the air and on the ground and for preserving the stories so others can learn from them.

Charles Rusk
October 27, 1932–April 3, 2017

Willard Rusk
October 12, 1921–October 1, 2003

Willard Rusk 1956 Cessna 195 NC4398N

Charles began by speaking of his 11-years-older brother Willard, who was born in Kansas and came to Valparaiso around 1950.[77] Willard and his wife Barbara adopted sons Tom and Cliff and then purchased a new house near the airport. Willard Rusk was the manager at Urschel Field and owner of Rusk Aviation. He had a crop-spraying operation using three Super Cubs with 150-horsepower engines. A regular Cub had about 100 horsepower. The tank with the chemicals sat behind the pilot. He instructed pilots, sold airplanes, and ran a charter service.

Charles said that crop dusting was not too dangerous, but you had to have the right amount of sleep. The pilots needed very light winds to be able to successfully do their job. They would get up around 4 a.m. and work all day until dark. If the winds stayed low, they would do this day after day. They usually sprayed cornfields and beanfields weekly within 30 miles of Urschel Field.

Charles was born in Beverly, Illinois. After he finished high school in 1950, he spent about three months working at the Urschel Field and also working at Nation Tube Co. in Gary, Indiana. He wanted to go into the Air Force but was told they were full up for pilots. He could have gone into the Navy, but that was of no interest to him. He went home and worked with his father for a while. Willard's best friend was a recruiter for the Air Force and got Charles into that branch, enabling him to learn all he could about aircraft maintenance. He moved into Willard's house

---

77. Phone conversation on December 1, 2012, and in person at Charles Rusk's home on February 8, 2013.

by the south hangar in June 1957 because Willard needed him to help with the work.

In August 1957 Charles said he had many days of beautiful flying weather. He flew almost every day at lunchtime to get his pilot's license. He usually flew in an Aeronca Champion. He used the GI Bill to get his license. He had his student pilot's license and quickly received his private pilot's license. Jim Slocum, who was even younger than Charles, was his instructor. Charles was Jim's first student. Jim started flying when he was seventeen at Urschel Field. One needed about 40 or 50 flying hours to get a private license. Charles kept flying, trying to obtain a commercial license. A minimum of 200 hours was required to get this license. He did a lot of this training in an Aeronca Champion and a Piper Tri-Pacer. He received this license in 1958; Keith Baird was his chief instructor.

Within six months, Charles acquired his flight instructor's license, which had required about an additional 20 or 30 hours of flying, including many hours of ground school. He wanted his flight instructor's license, so he could obtain more experience and earn more money. More experienced pilots had a much better chance of being hired by a major airline. Charles' favorite plane was an easy-to-fly, eight-passenger, twin-engine Piper Navajo.

A lot of the instructors at Urschel Field were busy earning money dusting, and Charles was getting a little impatient. He went to Chicago and finished all his training in short order, so he could get his instrument license. After he received this license, he would spend up to eight hours a day teaching. Many of these students wanted to work toward professional licenses. Rusk Aviation had a promoter who worked on getting students from other states. They ended up with students from all over the United States. When crop-spraying season started and the other pilots were busy, he had a heavy load of students demanding his time.

Charles had a student with whom he had a very close call. The student lost control of the plane during his first two landing attempts, so Charles took over. The next few attempts seemed a lot better, so Charles let him take off to land again. While the student was taking off, he started flying toward the planes that were tied down. Charles grabbed the controls and avoided the planes, but they were headed toward the T-hangars. He lifted the right wing over the hangar, and his left wing parted the gravel on the runway. Charles' legs shook as he finished the lesson; he couldn't believe they didn't crash.

An 1,800-ft. gravel runway, which ran parallel to the 2,600-ft. grass north-south runway was constructed at Urschel Field sometime in 1960. In the spring the grass runway was usually muddy as water drained to the middle. They had many students at this time and needed a runway that wasn't soggy. The 1,800-ft. east-west runway was seldom used except when there were strong crosswinds. Coming from the north and landing, a pilot had to be aware of how the field at the airport was constructed. This field rose at the north end, and then the ground dropped in the middle. A pilot would fly over all the trees, trying not to touch down on the high ground. They didn't want to have a flare-out, where they would have to pull the nose up.

Nine metal T-hangars were constructed at the field. A T-hangar is primarily used for private aircraft. The T-hangars can overlap one another and take up less room. The two most common configurations are the standard or stacked, shown below on the left, and the nested version on the right.[78]

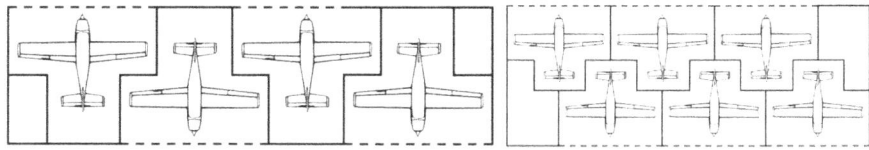

78. "Building a Hangar? Your Aircraft Hangar Design and Construction Guide." *Techspan.* https://techspanbuilding.com.au/articles/aircraft-hangar-design. Accessed 9 July 2023.

Airport activity slowed a little in the winter months, but it was still fairly busy. The men sometimes played ping-pong in the south hangar. Instruction went on as usual, and the shop was open from 8 a.m. to 5 p.m. during the week. At times instructors would come in and work on the planes. The metal mechanics building that Willard put up in front of the office held two planes that could be worked on simultaneously. When a plane had 100 hours of flying time, it was brought to the shop for maintenance, which included a complete visual inspection, oil change, and new spark

plugs. Charles mentioned if you were inspecting a Piper Tri-Pacer, you could pull the seat out of the front because it was on tracks. If the mechanic didn't fasten the seat down, the pilot would start sliding toward the back of the plane when taking off down the runway. The shop foreman was Bernie Rodgers.

Charles filled in details on why Urschel Field closed down even though it had been a vibrant, active place for so many people from the 1930s through the 1950s. First, in 1961 the north hangar burned to the ground, necessitating a rebuild. Gas from a leak on a crop-dusting plane had dripped on a moveable trouble light. Charles was in the office when Steve Kreshock saw the fire. Bernie Rodgers and everyone else ran to the hangar, but the plane was engulfed in flames by the time they arrived. They managed to get a plane or two out of the hangar; the rest burned. The loss was tremendous for Willard's company, as they also lost the trailer housing overhauled engines, a radio shop, and a great amount of lumber from Willard's closed lumber business. Willard moved his business to Kankakee, Illinois, along with his brother Charles and the radio repairman. Other instructors followed.

Charles thought the second reason Urschel Field closed was that he suspected Joe Urschel did not want to make any improvements on the property, as he intended to develop other things. Airplanes were getting bigger and faster, and those planes could not use a grass field. Space was not available for a long, hard surface runway. Charles said there were no hard feelings toward the Urschel Family.

Charles purchased an Aeronca Champion from his brother for $800. He stated that Cliff Magnor and Jim Slocum, both from Valparaiso, had trained at Urschel Field. They both were hired by different commercial airlines.

The conversation continued in person on February 8, 2013, at Charles and Patricia Rusk's house in Bradley, Illinois. Betty Kuehl, who worked

Charles and Pat Rusk

in the airport office, was also in attendance. Charles showed us his logbook, which had 683 hours of instructing student pilots.

He remembers his brother Willard putting a trailer on the road to the airport near Indiana Route 49 or Calumet Avenue around 1960. He advertised

and promoted Urschel Field nationwide, enticing students to come to Valparaiso. Chuck laughed when he recalled that the literature directed recruits to report to Room 102 since this room was the whole trailer. Students had to take 30 hours of ground school. Instructors included Keith Baird, Charles Younce, Steve Kreshock, Charles Rusk, and James Slocum. They were often required to teach when enrollment was high, even though most of them would rather have been crop dusting since it was more lucrative. Mechanics were Bernard Rodgers, Chuck Rader, and sometimes the pilots. The radio shop was managed by Steve Kreshock. Betty Kuehl, Willard Rusk, and daughter-in-law Patricia Rusk staffed the office.

Charles recalled he had two forced landings. His brother Willard had purchased two Aeronca Champions, and

Charles needed hours in a plane to obtain a license. His brother let him use one of these. It had wood frames covered with Irish linen. He was out practicing one day for his Certified Flight Instructor license and was at about 4,000 feet. At this time he was southwest of Urschel Field. The idle was set too low. He pulled the nose up to put it into a spin. The engine stopped, and he had to pick a decent field to glide into. He landed in a field where the timothy weed was up to his hips. He propped the plane and tried to take off but was unable to attain good speed because of the weeds. He kept trying, and on the fourth try, the plane took flight. He went under some wires, surprising himself that he cleared them. The guys at the field teased him since there were still many weeds covering the struts of his plane.

A couple of months later, he was flying near Porter County Airport, practicing for his commercial license. He was at about 500 feet. The engine sounded terrible, so he headed back to the airport, turned the key off, and the prop stopped instantly, freezing in position. He glided into the airport. The engine had swallowed the exhaust valve and had to be rebuilt.

Charles made money keeping the air stirred up over the fields. He said the higher-value crops, like potatoes, would be ruined if the temperature was too low. When a temperature inversion occurred, the pilots would stir the air to bring the warmer air down to the surface. Charles stated, "It helps if you are an idiot because it was dangerous work, and you flew all night. The money was good, usually double the rate of other work."

Another good aviation story begins on a Sunday when Willard had to fly a passenger to Benton Harbor, Michigan, in an Apache, which was a twin-engine Piper with a small carburetor heater, supposedly to keep the engine warm. Willard dropped his passenger off, and while heading back to Urschel Field, both of his engines began to slow down. The carburetor was icing, leaving him no choice but to land with gears up deep in snow drifts on a farmer's field. He walked to the farmer's house and eventually made it back to town. Willard recruited Charles, Bernie Rodgers, and Charley Vanderbilt to drive there to dig out the plane. With temperatures at 20 degrees below zero, they decided to postpone the trip. The next day it was still that cold, but they went with packed lunches since it was a long hike to the plane. A jack was used to get up under the plane. Due to the cold, work was done in short stints. They took a break and went to a restaurant, putting their hands under cold running water. Charles' right hand was always problematic in cold weather due to a prior frostbite. The retrieval process continued, and eventually, Keith Baird flew the plane home. A thousand rivets were used in repairing the plane's metal skin. This was the last plane they purchased with a small carburetor heater.

Charles finished his aviation memories recalling a somewhat goofy man who came to the airport to rent a plane. He would fly until he was almost out of gas, land in a farmer's field, and get free gas from the farmer, so he could keep flying. One time he fell asleep and woke up frightened. There was water all around him, as he was flying over Lake Michigan. Hopefully, that man learned his lesson.

Glenn Markley

August 8, 1933–August 7, 2021

Glenn lived in Chesterton and came to Valparaiso to see a huge air show featuring a biplane with a woman wing walker.[79] He also remembered some man taking off in his plane during the air show and almost hitting the biplane. After that show he decided that he wanted to get his license. He took lessons from H. H. Wait, Hugh Longnecker, and Claude Lindberg at Urschel Field. Glenn would go anywhere around northwest Indiana to get instruction and flight time. He said it cost him $3 an hour when he was doing solo flying and $6 with an instructor. Joe Phillips in Michigan City, Indiana, checked him out for his pilot's license.

Glen said that he called Urschel Field the "cereal bowl" because it was like flying into one from the north end of the runway that was elevated. He did a lot of slip practice coming in from the north end of the field. His friend would lend him his four-place Stinson Voyager to practice all his maneuvers as long as he paid for the gas and the maintenance. He used an Aeronca Champion that was owned by Willard Rusk and a Cub outfitted with skis owned by Mark Murvihill. That plane could land anywhere there was snow. Glenn leased planes from Murvihill after he moved to Porter County Airport. He would rent by the hour, taking off into the wind and coming back with a tailwind. He had only an hour and didn't want to be late coming back. He received his license in about 1958 or 1959 and quit flying shortly after that when he got married and started a family. In 1994 his grandchildren surprised him with an hour ride at Porter County Airport in a Cessna 172 trainer. He was hooked and once more started taking lessons, but he could not pass his physical since diabetes had diminished some of his eyesight.

He liked the Stinson airplane because it took off quickly and handled well. He felt very fortunate in that he flew many types of aircraft, especially a World War II T-6 and a T-34. His least favorite was a big and lumbering C-B amphibious plane that Joe Phillips owned.

He often used the Bodin Airport and would get his gas at Urschel Field or Porter County Airport. He thought the Bodin brothers were a little crazy; he mentioned that Sylven Bodin would come running toward the Stinson that Glenn and his buddy had just flown into the Bodin Airport.

---

79. Conversation at Glenn Markley's house.

Glenn's friend would get out of the airplane. Glenn would be in the back of the plane, and then Sylven would jump in and take off, saying he had to go check on some fields. Glenn was usually terrified when this happened because Sylven would fly so low that he could count the kernels on the corn. Sylven had no fear and was very uninhibited. Sylven thought he could do this since he owned the airport. To make matters worse, Sylven would get into the plane with manure on his boots.

He believed Guy Campolattara once saved him and his friend's life. They were going to land at a town near U.S. Routes 41 and 24. No light was on to tell them if the nose wheel had dropped down. The nose wheel worked on gravity. They circled and headed back to Porter County Airport. By the time they got back, Guy was already in the air, and both planes headed over to Kouts, Indiana, at about 4,000 feet. Guy demonstrated some maneuvers to try to get the nose wheel to come down. They tried for about 45 minutes and made four or five attempts, but it wasn't working. Guy put them through the maneuvers one more time, and it finally worked. Glenn's friend in the back seat was sick from all of the attempts to get the wheels down. Glenn thought he was relatively calm throughout the whole thing, but when they landed, he couldn't get out of the plane and needed help because he was thoroughly drained.

One time Glenn and his friend Chet Nunn took off from Bodin Airport, headed for South Bend, Indiana. The temperature was about 32 degrees, and they had gone through a lot of mud puddles on the runway before they were airborne. They arrived at South Bend and were told which runway to land on. The plane landed on the runway, the left gear touched, and suddenly they veered off sharply when the frozen wheel broke loose. The right gear suddenly broke free, and the plane almost did a ground loop. The tower asked them if this was normal for Porter County pilots. He told them "Yes."

Lawrence (Larry) Huber

February 8, 1943–

Lawrence Huber

Larry's father built a large yellow airplane windsock in this garage on McKinley Street for Urschel Field.[80] The tail would rotate, and the pilot would look at it to see which way the wind was blowing. Larry often would accompany his father to Urschel Field as the windsock was being installed.

Larry always wanted to learn to fly and earned money for flying lessons by mowing lawns. He did not remember his instructor's name when he started his lessons on April 26, 1959, as a sophomore in high school; however, he did remember that Bernard Bowen and Charles Younce gave him lessons from Urschel Field.

On August 22, 1959, he thought he was going to do a coordination exercise. He was flying with his instructor Bernard Bowen, doing landings and takeoffs. They landed on the south end of the runway, and Bernard got out. The temperature was 90 degrees outside, and inside the two-seat Champion, it was really hot. He was told to fly to Kouts, Indiana. Upon his return to Urschel Field, Larry was surprised to see that his parents and Bernard were out by the hangar to welcome him back from his first solo. On his landing he came in too fast from the north end of the runway. He revved his engine and came in for a second landing, this time just missing the high-tension wires by a couple of feet. He didn't know his parents had been notified by his instructor that he was going to solo.

On one occasion he came in with Bernard to land from the north end. His right wing tipped the ground due to the wind coming from the east-west runway causing the plane to take a 180-degree turn on the runway. Bernard looked at the hangars to see if anyone was looking and was thankful no one had seen this happen. Another day he and an instructor were flying in a Champion, and the instructor wanted Larry

80. Phone conversation with Larry Huber.

to do U-turns. The day was very hot, and Larry got dizzy and felt sick to his stomach, but he wouldn't let his instructor know.

He loved the airport and had fond memories of many flying antics, such as when his Aunt June was in Hebron, Indiana, hanging her laundry outside. Along came Bernard Bowen, flying very low. He killed the engine and then started it up again, which scared her. Although he took two more lessons after he had soloed, his last flight was on August 30, 1959, due to a lack of funds.

Larry Bub

March 24, 1937–

Larry's interest in aviation began in Pittsburgh, Pennsylvania, when he would talk with corporate pilots who were flying for MSA, the company that employed his dad.[81] Larry had begun studying engineering in college but left to get his aircraft mechanic's license at the Pittsburgh Institute of Aeronautics. After he earned his license in October 1961, he borrowed $100 from his parents and headed to Urschel Field because he had heard Urschel Field was looking for an airplane mechanic. He drove down the dirt road leading to Urschel Field and just sat there, somewhat dismayed, thinking the airport was going to be a much bigger operation. He didn't have the money to return home, so he figured he would stay until the following spring.

Larry stated that the airport school had students from all over the United States. There were no flying schools in the area except at Urschel Field. The south hangar at Urschel Field was used, as the north hangar had burned to the ground in 1961. Larry said the shop was really cold in the winter months. A house trailer was used to train the pilots. A club called "The Flying Squirrels" was formed to further aviation interests. Some of the pilots who worked at Urschel Laboratories flew secretly since Joe Urschel did not want any employees flying. These men were a tight group and never let it be known who might be flying.

Joe Urschel had an agreement with Willard Rusk that he could continue on the lease for the airport as long as people were using the airport. In 1962 Willard moved most of his operations to Kankakee, Illinois. A lot of pilots went with Willard to Kankakee. Many of these pilots would commute every day back to Urschel Field for crop dusting and such. Charles Younce and Bernie Rodgers were then put in charge of Urschel Field.

---

81. Conversations with Larry and Lois on November 2, 2012, December 3, 2012, and July 3, 2023.

Willard's secretary took over many tasks, so Willard was able to operate with a reduced staff. Larry and some of his friends came back to Valparaiso in 1963 and helped build a business called Professional Aviation, Inc. at Porter County Airport. Charles Younce was involved in the business in the early years. Eventually, Larry and Bernie Rodgers were partners until Bernie's retirement in 1995. They did crop dusting, sales, maintenance, etc. for more than 40 years. From 1995 through 2009, Larry also completed 306 annual plane inspections. He said he really, really missed all the guys, specifically naming Bernie Rodgers, Kenny Trulock, and Charles Younce. Larry also mentioned Edward Heath from New Buffalo, Michigan, who was a friend of William Urschel. At one time the Heath Company had built airplanes.

On May 23, 2012, Larry received the Charles Taylor Master Mechanic Award for his 50 years in the business. At that same ceremony Tom Cavanaugh received the Wright Brothers Master Pilot Award for demonstrating professionalism, skill, and aviation expertise. He credited Larry for maintaining his airplane and helicopter, stating, "He is the very best. He can repair anything and diagnose a problem very rapidly."

Jack Berkshire

July 29, 1940–October 28, 2013

Jack was born in North Judson, Indiana, but the family moved to La Crosse, Indiana, shortly thereafter.[82] Flying was something he thought about as a young boy. In 1956 at age fifteen, he was determined to somehow get to Urschel Field. His family was still living in La Crosse, a large farming community. He earned money at the City Service filling station that Ray Heinhold owned. Jack earned about 75 cents an hour.

A friend named Ron was six months older. Ron had a car, and he also wanted to learn how to fly, so the two of them would come to Urschel Field when they had enough money for a lesson. When Jack was sixteen, he purchased a 1950 Ford.

Charles Rusk was the first of Jack's four flight instructors. Charles taught him to do spins after just a few hours in the air. He would stall the plane, and it would come down spinning, so he had to practice getting out of the spins. To solo, a pilot had to know how to get out of a spin. Another instructor was Charles Younce, who trained in an Aeronca Champion 7AC. In 1956 after only six hours in the air, Jack soloed. He had to fly to Michigan City, Indiana, with his instructor to get the correct papers that would allow him to solo. After the third attempt of trying to find Joe Phillips Airport in Michigan City, he finally had the necessary paperwork completed.

When pilots solo for the first time, they are supposed to stay in a pattern. Jack was expected to fly near Urschel Field and practice doing takeoffs and landings. He decided to do something different. He took off for La Crosse, hoping to see his father. He spotted him by the Pennsylvania Railroad tower and buzzed him. His dad was actually able to see Jack. Upon landing back at Urschel Field, Jack said he caught all kinds of hell because he was supposed to stay in the pattern. He can't remember now if he knew that or not, but he didn't care because he wanted his dad to see him.

---

82. Phone conversation on December 3, 2012.

Sometimes he would wait months between lessons because he needed to earn extra money. He had to pay $8 per hour to rent a plane plus an additional $4 if an instructor went along. He loved being at Urschel Field, where there was a great group of people and many old training airplanes.

In 1962 he earned his private pilot's license at Porter County Airport in a two-passenger high-wing Piper Colt. He was married and didn't have a lot of extra money. He flew a lot from Urschel Field and recalled one time landing a Cessna 180 on the east-west runway because of the winds. That runway wasn't used very often as it was shorter than the north-south runway. He also mentioned the "Bamboo Bomber" that they kept in the north hangar. It was a Cessna twin-engine made of wood and covered in fabric. One final memory concerning Urschel Field was that during World War II, P-51s would sometimes land there.

Jack thought highly of Charles Younce, who was a crop duster as well as an instructor; he admired the mechanical skills of Bernie Rodgers.

A promoter who Willard Rusk hired flew a Tri-Pacer around the country. Jack thought this was about 1960. He was trying to recruit students for the school that Willard had started. The tuition was $3,200, but it covered multi-engine, instrument, instructor, private, and commercial licenses.

His love of aviation provided a rewarding and interesting career, as he ended up flying for United Air Lines from May 1966 to August 1, 2000. He was stationed for a little while in San Francisco but did most of his flying out of O'Hare Airport in Chicago.

John Roberts
November 28, 1948–

John grew up at 701 Glendale Ave, Valparaiso, Indiana. John had many memories of Urschel Field, as his house was just south of the runway.[83] He stated it as "off the berm" of the north-south runway. The planes would come in and take off over his house all day long. He loved planes from his earliest memories. He recalls running through the cornfields to sit on a hill where he could watch all the activity at the airport. Most of the planes were covered with fabric. At the dope and fabric shop, the fabric was covered with chemicals, and the fumes would waft up toward him as he was sitting on the hill, observing all the activity.

One day John went to the airport and walked up to the hangars. Someone asked him what he was doing, and he stated that he wanted to take a ride. He was about five years old. He had $7 in his hand to pay for the flight. A pilot from the Rusk Flying Service told him they would have to call his parents. They said it was fine, and up he went for a 30-minute ride in a Piper Cub. They had him sit on some phone books so he could see out the window.

He received his pilot's license while he was in high school before he got his driver's license. He soloed in a Cessna 150 at Porter County Airport. After graduating from high school in 1967, he received a degree in aviation technology from Purdue University. He always wanted to know all about airplanes and how they worked. He flew many kinds of aircraft in his life. One that he didn't care for was the V-Tailed Beechcraft Bonanza because it caused pilot fatigue. He also said that the Piper Tri-Pacer was nicknamed "Falling Rocks," as it had no glide ratio.

John mentioned that Charlie Younce flew low over the fields for crop dusting. Charlie told him it was because he got nosebleeds if he went above 3,000 feet. His last anecdote was of Mark Murvihill, who John thought was a very kind and decent man.

---

83. Phone conversation on December 30, 2012.

Aviation in Porter County, Indiana
The Early Decades

1896 Jun   Octave Chanute, who lived in Chicago, came to the Indiana Dunes, notably Miller Beach in Lake County and Waverly Beach in Porter County, to experiment with flying his gliders. His book *Progress in Flying Machines* was published in 1894. He invented the "strut wire" braced-wing structure used in powered biplanes. His gliders also used multiple wings. The Wright brothers conferred with him on many occasions.

1911 Aug   Chicagoan Harry Olson shipped a Wright biplane to Chesterton and kept it at the Shaner barn. Harry's grandfather was long-time Chesterton resident Charles Lawrence.

1912 May   Harry Olson flew the biplane successfully from Lindeman's field at 5th and Porter Avenue in Chesterton. Harry Olson kept his Farman and Curtiss biplane at Lindeman's field. He left Chesterton after being offered a contract to become a barnstormer.

1913 Jun   Emerson Cota from Valparaiso had two successful glider flights at the Clifford farm in Chesterton, rising to 150 feet. He flew an 18-foot glider patterned after the Wright Brothers' glider. Emerson left to join the Navy and served six years.

1913 Jul   Tony Jannus flew his plane at Flint Lake in Valparaiso. Due to the lake's small size, he had trouble getting airborne and mostly just skimmed the lake. He managed to get his plane in the air, just once, barely over the trees around the lake.

1917 Sep Katherine Stinson crashed her Curtiss biplane on the Schultz farm in Chesterton. Having earned her pilot's license in 1912, she was the first to fly mail by air between Calgary and Edmonton in Canada, the first female to fly the U.S. mail, and the first person to do skywriting. She also established an airport in San Antonio, Texas, that is named after her.

1919 Jun The first air-freight consignment in Porter County was a shipment of clothes from Chicago to Lowenstine's store in Valparaiso. The flight took 25 minutes.

1919 Jul Two planes landed in a field in Chesterton; one had run low on gas. They were headed to Chicago after entertaining crowds in Toledo for the Willard-Dempsey fight.

1920 Lt. W. J. Smith landed a mail plane in a field on the Morgan farm due to heavy fog. The field was too muddy for takeoff, so the plane was dismantled and shipped by train to Chicago.

1920 Farr Nutter crashed a mail plane on the Ralph Peterson farm. Farr was not injured and later flew the mail route from San Francisco, California, to Reno, Nevada. The mail was loaded on the train and sent to Chicago.

1921 Jack Knight, a World War I pilot and an aerobatic flying instructor, was the first to fly the mail at night. His flight demonstrated the feasibility of flying the mail at night and led Congress to support the airmail program. The trip was from Omaha to Chicago. He lived in Dune Acres in Porter County. When he died in 1945, he had flown 2,400,000 miles. He worked for United Airlines and was one of their first pilots.

1923	William Quase settled in Chesterton from Chicago and was friends with Raymond and Henry DeMass. He instructed students in his Jenny biplane. He had been a World War I pilot.
1923	The federal government listed three emergency airfields in Porter County:

- Burdick, near the depot and the church steeple
- Crisman 2000′ x1200′ W of PO between RR Crocker by USTI (no location given)
- McCool Airport Chi-N.Y. Airway #3 Int Elevation 654 Lat 41.43 Long -87.09. This airfield was on Glen Robbins' property about a half mile north of the second McCool Airport on U.S. Route 6.

1923	Henry DeMass of Chesterton enrolled in Culver Military Academy's two-year aviation program. After one year that program ended because the school found it impractical to continue.
1925	The Chesterton Airport at 5th and Porter was established as an official airport. The Duffy family used this field. The Duffys had a few planes; one was a World War I French Newport fighter plane, which had a rotating engine.
1925	The Ford School of Aviation opened at the Chesterton Airport. The tuition for a complete aviation course was $100, while a ride was just $3.
1925	Brothers Henry and Raymond DeMass hired John Brown from Kankakee, Illinois, to instruct them in flying. The brothers were considered by many to be the original aviation enthusiasts in Porter County.
1926	William Urschel purchased the farm where Urschel Field would soon be located.

1927	Oakley Lutes piloted the American Eagle plane owned by Chesterton resident Carl Harvil to pick up Carl's adopted twins from a Chicago orphanage. The twins, named "George Frederick" and "Frederick George," were three years old.
1927 Aug	William Quase, a World War I pilot and instructor, was killed in an air crash over Oak Lawn, Illinois.
1928	C. Lee Nelson of Valparaiso built a small hangar near Hall's factory on State Road 49 just east of Urschel Field and a mile north of the old fairgrounds. He received his private pilot's license in a Waco 10.
1928 May	Russell Hankforth flew Carl and Vaughn Harvil from Chesterton to Indianapolis for the 16th International 500-Mile Sweepstakes Race. This trip took two hours in his three-place Laird Swallow.
1928 Jun	Russell Hankforth advertised in the paper: "Flying School - Chesterton, Indiana. Student training, passenger flights, and commercial licenses. We can back you in 6 to 8 weeks."
1928 Jul	William Urschel, Glen Goddard, and Vaughn Harvil had a Swallow plane brought to Valparaiso for inspection, but they did not purchase it. The trio had the intention of getting a flying field established.
1929	McCool Airport, with a beacon and a small building, was established on Airport Road and U.S. Route 6 as a government field for emergency landings of mail planes. McCool Airport was plowed under in 1948.

1929 Mar	Committee "H," consisting of J. F. Griffin, M. F. French, Vaughn Harvil, Mayor Leetz, and William Urschel, was formed to find a way to secure a proper landing field in Valparaiso.
1929 Jun	The French Motor Company sponsored a 25-minute ride in a Ford all-metal Tri-Motor giant airliner at Urschel Field for $5.
1929 Jun	A Ford Tri-Motor was flown to Urschel Field from Goshen, Indiana. William Urschel, Mayor Leetz, Chamber of Commerce president T. L. Applegate, J. William Bosse, H. M. Evans, Harry Arnold, and two others were passengers. The plane was mired in the mud after landing at Urschel Field. Five hundred people were on hand to see the landing. Hundreds had hoped to take a ride. They were directed to Knox, Indiana, the following day to take their prepaid rides.
1929 Aug	C. Lee Nelson, a licensed pilot, received his limited commercial license, hoping to make aviation his lifework. C. Lee offered sightseeing trips on a field a mile north of the old Valparaiso fairgrounds. The cost was $2.50 for two passengers and $3 for a single passenger.
1929 Aug	William Urschel, Carl Harvil, Vaughn Harvil, and The Charles Pratt American Legion Post in Valparaiso unsuccessfully tried to get the city interested in establishing an airport.
1929 Aug	Oakley Lutes offered plane rides from a field opposite Graceland Cemetery on U.S. Route 30 for the same amount as C. Lee Nelson.
1929 Aug	Henry and Raymond DeMass had the motors stolen from their Jenny and Canuck biplanes at Chesterton Airport.

1929 Sep	McCool Airfield was named one of Indiana's 10 best intermediate landing fields.
1929 Oct	Jesse L. Gross, from South Bend, Indiana, offered flights over the Dunes from the Chesterton Airport. He flew with his friend Claude Lindberg in 1924. He was one of the first to purchase a plane from Lindberg.
1929 Oct	Carl and Vaughn Harvil remodeled a barn at Chesterton Airport to become a hangar for their American Eagle plane. Noted in the paper: "Jesse Gross will fly the Harvil brothers' plane next Sunday."
1929	Chesterton resident Russell Hankforth, nicknamed "Fred Fearnot," flew for the Harvils. Russell took Pearl Linderman for a ride, and upon landing, the engine fell off the plane. In anger he just threw the engine over the fence. Later that plane burned up when a welder with a torch was working on it.
1930	Bud Winder established an airport on the Evans' field south of U.S. Route 30 across from what is now Porter County Airport. He planned to build a hangar in the future. He used this field until 1934 when he moved all operations to Urschel Field.
1930 May	Carl Harvil and his wife Lou flew to Indianapolis to watch the Indianapolis 500-Mile Race and returned immediately after the race. Jesse Gross piloted the plane for them.
1930 Jul	Art Loeffel, a daredevil from Universal Company, jumped from 1,500 feet during a fairground program. The plane departed from C. Lee Nelson's field, piloted by Jesse Gross.
1930 Jul	Indiana Governor Leslie's son Richard was given a plane ride from the Chesterton Airport.

1930 Aug   The Chesterton Airport official grand opening was going to be celebrated with champagne until the Woman's Christian Temperance Union objected. Instead, cars were driven around the field three times by Chamber of Commerce members to dedicate the field.

1930 Aug   A six-place Bellanca cabin monoplane with a 425-horse-power motor landed at C. Lee Nelson's field.

1930 Nov   A rum-laden plane was seized in Columbia, Mississippi, with Russell Hankforth suspected as the pilot.

1931 Jun   Valparaiso was chosen as a stop on the 25-plane Big Squadron air tour. William Urschel headed the Chamber of Commerce airport committee and was instrumental in getting Valparaiso placed on the schedule.

The first man on the left is unidentified, then Henry Foster, Dick Villiume, Olie Sundelin, Ralph Barneko, Bus Babcock, Bun Blackman, Bud Winder, Mark Murvihill, and the last two men could not be identified. Circa 1931

1931 Jun   Several thousand people who lined the highways around Urschel Field to see the air tour were very disappointed. Urschel Field was too soft and soggy due to recent rains, and only six planes were able to land. The others were flagged to Michigan City, Indiana.

1931 Jul   Chesterton native Russell Hankforth did a show of aerial acrobatics in his hometown. He also flew out of Omaha as an airmail pilot. He moved to Hollywood to act/fly in movies. He was the pilot in the 1931 film *Flying High*.

1931 Aug   Glen Goddard wanted the city to take action immediately to establish an airport. William Urschel, Glen Goddard, and others believed the field on Dr. H. M. Evans' farm was the best in the vicinity. The financial aid from the city for the project was not forthcoming.

1931 Sep   Claude Lindberg offered rides for $1 on V. B. Clevenger's farm, Babcock Station, Indiana.

1931 Nov   "Broncho" John Sullivan, one of the few remaining Indian scouts, was given a ride by Bud Winder over the city. Bud kept his plane at C. Lee Nelson's field. Bud planned to erect a hangar on his field 2.5 miles east of Valparaiso south of U.S. Route 30.

1932 Feb   Russell Hankforth and seven other men's conspiracy trial started in a federal court in Biloxi, Mississippi. They had been charged following the November 10, 1930, seizure in Columbia, Mississippi, of their plane transporting cases of rum. Prosecutors believed Hankforth was piloting the plane and was a part of a liquor-running syndicate. All were acquitted due to lack of evidence.

1932 Sep   Bud Winder received his air transport license and began giving rides from his airport in October.

1933 Mar   Bud Winder organized a glider aero club at his airfield.

1933 Jun   George Varga, an Indiana champion parachute jumper, practiced at the Winder Airport.

1933 Jul   Bud Winder carried passenger Rollie Humphrey in his one-place glider. Others in the Valparaiso Aero Club who flew gliders that day were Bob Lenberg, Stub Lenberg, Axel Nogard Jr., and Olie Sundelin. Bud also flew a new cabin plane. He invited the public to his airport.

1933 Oct   A United Air Lines plane crashed in Jackson Township, killing all seven people on board. Some believed a bomb had been placed in the baggage compartment, which if true made it the first act of terrorism in the United States.

1933 Dec   Glen Goddard and William Urschel presented documentation to the Valparaiso City Council showing the U.S. government was willing to grant monies to public airports for improvements, necessitating the city to take ownership of Urschel Field.

1934 Jan   To be able to receive federal funding, Valparaiso City Council adopted an ordinance to enter into a five-year lease with William Urschel for a 60-acre tract at Wolf's Corners on State Road 49 with the option of purchasing this land. The airport was to be known as the Valparaiso Municipal Airport. About 50 men under the Civil Works Administration (CWA) began to level the field. Bud Winder was the manager of this airport.

1934 Feb   Mayor Harold Schenck officially signed the ordinance for the five-year lease, and the city was informed that $12,000 would be made available by the state to be expended for CWA labor used to prepare the field.

1934 May   Bud Winder closed his airport and relocated his operations to Urschel Field. Bud became the manager of Urschel Field.

1934   Valpo Aero Club was formed in Valparaiso with 12 members flying gliders.

1935 Feb   Glen Goddard stated there was no foundation to the rumor that he expected to fly passengers over the nudist colony.

1935 Apr   Glen Goddard purchased a Stinson plane to be housed at the Gary Airport. Urschel Field did not yet have a large enough hangar.

1935 Jun   Urschel Field was considered a municipal airport at this time since the city was leasing it. The city was divided on helping the airport. William Urschel and the Aero Club wanted the city to donate Lincolnway paving bricks to build a hangar. Urschel proposed a plan to the council that he would forego the money for the lease agreement the following year to help pay for the bricks. All negotiations fell through.

1935 Jun   Bud Winder, Glen Goddard, and William Younce traveled to Rensselaer, Indiana, to present an air circus. They wanted Urschel Field completed, so this could be performed in Valparaiso.

1935 Jul   Glen Goddard actively promoted moving McCool Airport emergency landing operations to Urschel Field because Urschel Field was less susceptible to dense fog and had longer runways. This did not happen.

1935 Sep   Claude Lindberg was elected president of Aero Club. The club's Waco glider was flown on the weekends.

1935 Nov   The city was advised that they must acquire the 60 acres that they were leasing from William Urschel.

1936   The Bureau of Aeronautics in Washington, DC, ruled that no more government monies would be given to upgrade Urschel Field. A $47,000 grant was contingent on Urschel Field becoming a municipal airport with the city owning the land. William Urschel, Glenn Goddard, and others continued working with the city to facilitate the process of transferring ownership and responsibility to the city.

1936 Feb   Members of a special committee outlined methods by which the city could obtain the Urschel Field land.

1936 Mar   City lagged on airport plans.

1936   The Valparaiso Aero Club had 23 members: Bud Winder, Claude Lindberg, C. Lee Nelson, Bill Younce, Olie Sundelin, Henry Foster, Daniel Perry, Ben Blackman, Bun Blackman, Axel Nogard Jr., Arthur Babcock, Harrold McCray, Hillary Dunn, Chuck Lucas, Ralph Barneko, Clarence Powell, Mark Murvihill, Fred Giroux, Kenneth Busier, Richard Williams, Buster Babcock, Bus Babcock, and Dr. Van Winkel.

1936 May   Claude Lindberg, Bud Winder, Axel Nogard Jr., Olie Sundelin, and Henry Foster of the Aero Club purchased a WOW training plane in Chicago. This plane was kept in Chicago until a hangar was built at the airfield.

1936 May   Glen Goddard, local agent for American Airlines, said people could book passage on the Airship Hindenburg, which would arrive in America that morning. The one-way fare was $400, and the round trip was $750. Special trips were being made for the Summer Olympic Games held in Germany. Did someone forget to tell the paper to pull the ad?

1936 Sep Six planes were quartered at the airport: Bud Winder's Waco 10, Bill Younce and Bob Lenberg's Eaglerock, Valparaiso Aero Club's Waco 10, Rex McNeely's Swallow, C. Lee Nelson's Waco 10, and S. Braden's Monocoupe. Only one plane could be in the hangar at a time.

1936 Oct Aero Club gave an air show consisting of stunt flying, ribbon cutting, bombing a moving car, dead-stick landing, and other entertainment. All flyers were local and no admission was charged.

1936 Dec William Urschel and 20 members of the Valparaiso Aero Club came before the City Council and called for a showdown on what the city desired. The city could break the lease and buy the airfield from Urschel to comply with the federal government's funding requirement. The other option would have been to revert the airport to a private airfield, canceling the planned improvements. William stated he purchased the land in 1926 intending to subdivide it. He became interested in flying and in the Valparaiso Aero Club, which now had about 30 members. The city did not want to expend any more money. The lease was canceled in January 1937. Urschel Field became a private airport again.

1937 Feb Bud Winder leased Urschel Field. He raised money by having air shows and operating a flying service.

1937 Jun Forty-eight planes participating in the Ninth Annual Indiana Air Tour were forced down when flying from Gary to Michigan City, Indiana. A dense fog quickly enveloped them, and they landed wherever they could. The ceiling was reduced from 1,200 feet to zero in a few minutes. All planes landed safely.

1937 Aug   An estimated 10,000 people witnessed the Linco Aces air show at Urschel Field as they jammed country lanes to get there. Lt. J. C. Mackey flew

Various photos from the 1937 Urschel Field air show.

his special Waco Taperwing at 300 miles an hour. Also to appear was the "bat-wing" jumper, Earl Stein. He was taken to 14,000 feet and dropped more than 2 miles in his special suit. There were dogfights and much more. The Linco Aces were considered the premier barnstorming group, as each of them had won numerous awards.

1937 Sep   Claude Lindberg was elected president of Valparaiso Aero Club. Members were flying a Waco biplane.

1938 Jul   Local flyers thrilled many in the First Annual Air Tour sponsored by the Northern Indiana Pilots' Council. All the planes stopped at several NW Indiana airports and ended with an air show at Urschel Field.

1938 Jul   Devil Dog Air Show performed in Valparaiso. Many of their stunts had never been performed at other air shows.

1938 Aug   The Valparaiso Aero Club took a day off for a get-together, picnic, and aviation contest. Some who participated in the contest were Bud Winder, Rollie Humphrey, Art

Babcock, Ralph Barneko, Bus Babcock, Clarence Fisher, Irv Shaffer, Rollie Fischer, Olie Sundelin, Henry Foster, Bun Blackman, Steve Noble, Dick Villiume, Axel Nogard Jr., and Joe Urschel.

1938 Aug Nena Winder Babcock, 16, became the first woman from Porter County to solo at Urschel Field. She was the younger sister of Bud Winder.

1938 Sep Work progressed on a 10- to 12-plane hangar at Urschel Field with completion expected the following year.

1938 Oct Marty Rintz of Chesterton crashed the plane he had built using various scrap parts.

1938 Oct Olie Sundelin and Bun Blackman were severely injured when their plane crashed east of Boone Grove.

1938 Dec Valparaiso Aero Club members observed Aviation Day with a banquet celebrating the thirty-fifth anniversary of the Wrights' Kitty Hawk flight. Being honored were Bud Winder and William Urschel for supporting the Valparaiso Aero Club since its formation. More than 150 aviation enthusiasts attended.

1939 Feb "Airport Activity" column debuted in *The Vidette-Messenger* newspaper.

1939 Feb Steve Noble had a grand opening of his remodeled Coney Island Sandwich Shop at 51 South Michigan. Steve was a member of the Valparaiso Aero Club.

1939 Apr Oakley Lutes purchased another plane, a Warner-powered Stinson. Oakley held one of the first licenses the Bureau of Air Commerce issued.

1939 May   Oakley Lutes broke the altitude record for the airport at 15,000 feet. The temperature was below freezing.

1939 Jun   A fierce tornadic windstorm and torrential rains wreaked havoc on Porter County. Urschel Field's 9-plane hangar was damaged, the planes were wrecked, and a small house was destroyed. Both were rebuilt. Another small hangar owned by the Valparaiso Aero Club and the two planes inside were totaled.

1939 Aug   From Urschel Field Mrs. H. H. Wait of Chesterton and her two sons Horatio and Sears began the first leg of their 23,000-mile trip around the world with stops in Honolulu, Hong Kong, Bangkok, Rangoon, Karachi, Cairo, Tunis, Paris, London, and home via a Pan-American clipper. They were stranded close to Hong Kong when World War II broke out, but they eventually returned home.

1939 Aug   Thousands came to see the Valparaiso Air Show at Urschel Field.

1939 Dec   A large crowd attended the Valparaiso Aero Club Aviation Day Banquet. Headliners were Jack Knight, who flew the first nighttime airmail flight, and John Wilson, dean of aeronautics at the Holy Name School in Lockport, Illinois. Dr. Van Winkle, the medical examiner for the Valparaiso Aero Club, presided over the banquet. Many people were introduced, including Speed Chandler, a famous auto racer; William Urschel, called the "godfather" of the club; C. Lee Nelson and Oakley Lutes as the oldest flyers in terms of when they began flying.

1940 Ruth Robbins earned her pilot's license at Urschel Field. She was a plane partner with Mark Murvihill.

1940 May A building used as an office and a clubhouse was completed next to the hangar at Urschel Field.

1940 Jun Valparaiso University, in conjunction with the Winder Flying Service at Urschel Field, offered a free 12-week primary course in aviation. The government course complied with President Roosevelt's plea for training 50,000 civilian pilots.

1940 Jun Seventy-five men were flying regularly at Urschel Field. Among them, 2 held instructors' licenses, 4 were commercial pilots, 9 were private pilots, and 37 were taking instruction. Others came regularly from other fields.

1940 Aug   Bette Nogard Richards soloed at Urschel Field.

1940 Aug   Lt. John "Bud" Winder of the U.S. Army Reserve Air Corps flew low over downtown Valparaiso in a BT-9 with a 400-horsepower engine.

1940 Oct   Urschel Field had two large hangars that could hold 12 planes each. The airport housed 18 planes. Approximately 1,440 student flying hours and 1,000 hours by private pilots were chalked up that summer. About 2,500 passengers were flown by airport staff, using about 15,500 gallons of gas.

1941 Jan   Axel Nogard Jr., Robert Ulsh, Lawrence Gesse, and Arthur Babcock left Urschel Field for Miami, Florida, as participants in that city's annual Light Airplane Cavalcade.

1941 Feb   Lieutenant Bud Winder sold Winder Flying Service at Urschel Field to Henry Foster and Olie Sundelin. Bud and his family moved to Santa Monica, California, to become an inspector for the Civil Aeronautics Administration (CAA).

1941 Mar   Flight instruction in the third CAA program began at Valparaiso University in conjunction with Urschel Field. Bette Nogard Richards was enrolled in this third program. All students in the first two classes had passed.

1941 Apr   Axel Nogard Jr. became a CAA inspector and reported to CAA headquarters at LaGuardia Field in New York City.

1941 Apr   Steve Noble and several other Porter County airmen joined the Canadian Royal Air Force.

1941 Dec	The national organization Civil Air Patrol (CAP) was founded.
1942 Apr	A B-25 belly-crashed after striking a telephone pole near McCool Airport.
1942 Jul	Urschel Field was managed by The Valparaiso Aero Club, one of the oldest clubs in Indiana.
1942 Dec	Colonel Roscoe Turner, internationally famed speed flier, was the main speaker at the CAP Banquet.
1943 Aug	Pilot Officer of the Royal Canadian Air Force Steven Noble was killed flying a bombing mission over Germany. His plane was christened "Miss Valparaiso" after his home city.
1944	Valparaiso's Urschel Field, with seven other airports and cities nationwide, was included in a Civil Aeronautics Administration (CAA) study for funding existing and new airports. Engineers surveyed all possible sites. Urschel Field was not selected to receive money from the CAA.
1944 Jun	Bette Nogard Richards graduated from the Women Airforce Service Pilot (WASP) program in Sweetwater, Texas. She was the only WASP from Porter County.
1944 Jul	Most of the CCC Camp buildings were taken away. "They will be replaced at a future time with a grand park and buildings suitable to the splendid Air City we will always call Urschel Field," quoted a city official.
1944 Sep	Ruth Robbin's Aeronca was returned to her after being used in the war to train pilots.
1944 Oct	Mobil Oil painted large signs on hangars to identify Urschel Field.

1944 Nov	Civil Air Patrol leased a T-shaped building at Urschel Field for ground instruction, drill classes, and other activities.
1945 Jul	The Porter County Aviation Committee was formed to get ideas for developing a county airport to meet future needs.
1945 Jul	In a Stinson airplane Olie Sundelin flew William Urschel to Columbus, Ohio, in two hours and twenty minutes. This was William's first long-distance flight. Coming back, William's train ride was nine hours.
1945 Aug	Carrying 13 people, a DC-3 left Urschel Field problem-free.
1945 Sep	Two Chesterton boys hid in an Urschel Field hangar and later in the night took off with Chesterton Aero Club's Piper Cub. They flew the plane without lights and landed at the South Bend Airport when their fuel was nearly depleted. They walked away and hitchhiked back home. The pilot, Ronnie Smalley, 15, had some hours in a plane, but he did not have a license.
1945 Oct	The non-profit Valparaiso Aero Club was dissolved and replaced by a profit organization. This was revealed by the new president of the aviation firm, Claude Lindberg. They then started selling Luscombe aircraft. Urschel Field contained about 100 acres, with about 125 more acres available from William Urschel.
1947 Sep	The Valparaiso Aero Club, Inc. was sold to Earl and Emma Green and George Wiemuth. Martin Young succeeded Claude Lindberg as president of the firm.
1948	The U.S. Department of Commerce terminated its lease of 57 acres at McCool Airport with the exception of the land that held the beacon. The airport had been used as an emergency landing field. McCool Airport was plowed

under. Unable to find any parties interested in buying the property, owner Ross Crisman decided to use the land for farming.

1948   Maury Anderson, Arthur Babcock, and Olie Sundelin began construction of the Knight Twister in Olie's basement. It was completed in 1950.

1948 Sep   William E. Urschel died on September 7.

1948 Dec   Indiana Aeronautics Commission awarded a national certificate to Urschel Field for good operating practices.

1949   Porter County Airport was established. Its grand opening was in 1950, and it was dedicated in the spring of 1951.

1950   In the early 1950s Urschel Field was listed in an aviation magazine as the busiest privately held airport in the country.

1950 Jul   Ken Wyckoff, president of the Flying Farmers of Prairieland, stated there were 725 planes in Chicago for the dedication of Meigs Field. The Flying Farmers came from 34 states.

1951 Aug   Fifty-two students were enrolled in lessons at Urschel Field using the GI Bill, plus two private students.

Stinson airplane at Urschel Field in the early 1950s.

1952 May   Runway lights were installed on the 2,650-foot north-south runway at Urschel Field. Night flying lessons were started.

1952 Aug   Three Valparaiso men died in a P-13 Vultee plane crash: Pilot Joseph Cook, Benny Ripley, and Wendell Stoner. The CAA inspector said they were stunting too close to the ground.

1953 Sep   The Knight Twister participated in the first Experimental Aircraft Association's (EAA) fly-in convention in Milwaukee, Wisconsin. There were 21 planes and about 150 people in attendance.

1953 Sep   A National Guard unit prepared a parking area for 20,000 cars. An estimated 12,000 people attended the air show—6,000 inside the airport and another 6,000 outside the field. A storm in the middle of the program caused the military planes to be canceled. The National Aerobatic Champions of the World, the Cole Brothers, performed. The show continued after the storm. A headline in *The Vidette-Messenger* incorrectly stated this was the first air show held at Urschel Field. However, an article published on August 8, 1937, reported that 10,000 people had attended an Urschel Field air show.

1953 Oct   Chuck Hoover flew the Knight Twister to the Chicago O'Hare Air Show. He began scraping 5-foot weeds on takeoff, so he brought the craft down and landed it. The wheel was slightly damaged, causing him to withdraw. The plane had a 15-foot wingspan and was the only midget in the show.

1954 Jan   Urschel Field began using adjustable stretchers for medical patients, permitting time-saving plane transportation. The air ambulance was used 12 times in the first month.

1954 Jun   Irene Leverton crashed a PA-18A (8178C) while crop dusting for Willard Rusk in La Crosse, Indiana. She reported crop dusting was the most lucrative job she ever had. She was a member of the Ninety-Nines International Organization of Women Pilots and was a Mercury 13 astronaut candidate. In her lifetime she flew more than 25,000 hours and received multiple awards for various aviation feats.

1955 Jul   McCool Airport's beacon, lights, and markers were moved to Porter County Airport.

```
(1955)  Piper Cub   N78623
        Color: Yellow & Blue
```

1956   Nike Missile System C-47 base, started in 1954, was completed near Wheeler, Indiana.

1956 Apr   Willard Rusk asked permission to erect a 10-plane T- hangar at Urschel Field.

1956 Apr   Chicagoans Gordon and Josephine Blake were killed on the Wayne Michaels' farm, just northwest of Valparaiso. They were heading home in a snowstorm after meeting with Willard Rusk to purchase a larger plane.

1957 Jan   Dr. Arthur J. Van Winkle died. Dr. Van Winkle was the physician for the pilots' medical exams and the author of the Urschel Field newspaper column which appeared in *The Vidette-Messenger*. He was a great supporter and friend of all involved in aviation.

1958 Sep Twelve students who had never flown formed the Flying Aces Club and pooled their money to buy an Aeronca Champion. Nine soloed shortly thereafter. Other clubs at Urschel Field were the Tri-Pacer Club, the Blue Birds, the Skyways, and the Sportsmen.

1960 Jan Valparaiso School of Aeronautics opened at Urschel Field and enrolled 71 students.

1961 Feb The north hangar at Urschel Field burned to the ground, which was a tremendous loss. Two planes were totaled, while several others were pulled to safety. Willard Rusk stated that Rusk Aviation, Inc. at Urschel Field would continue to operate. Charles Younce finished instruction with several students. By 1962 Rusk had moved most parts of his operation to Kankakee, Illinois.

1963 Mar Charles Younce still taught at Urschel Field. He also operated a crop-dusting service, a charter service, and a repair shop.

1963 Oct Pilot Louis Wyckoff and passenger Leslie Weimer crashed a Cessna 182 into the side of a mountain in Wyoming. Willard Rusk and Robert Bartholomew flew from Urschel Field to Wyoming to pick up the bodies but were prevented from recovering them due to winter weather conditions.

Late 1963 After 30 years of operation, Urschel Field closed. Large Xs were placed on the field. Most pilots and mechanics moved to Porter County Airport or Kankakee, Illinois.

1964 Jul The last piece of equipment from Urschel Field was removed by Willard Rusk on July 1, 1964.

Acknowledgments

In researching the stories of early aviation in Porter County, information was gathered from the following sources:

The Vidette-Messenger
The Chesterton Tribune
Newspaper.com
Ancestry.com
Findagrave.com
Inportercounty.org
Portage Community Historical Society
WASP Museum Sweetwater, Texas
Kevin Pazour, Porter County Museum Valparaiso
Eva Hopkins, Westchester Township History Museum
Larry Clark, Porter County Genealogy Department
Nancy Vaillancourt, historian and researcher
Russ Ryle, historian
Bernie Rodgers, photographer
Joyce Hicks, publishing resource
All of the pilots and their families

Notes

Cover painting by Thad Hackett. In 1963 Betty Kuehl-Heffner rescued the cover painting from a trash can before Urschel Field was demolished. Betty remembered that the painting had been gifted to Bud as he left Valparaiso for his new career in California. When the backing was taken off, the following text, imprinted into a wooden stretcher bar, was discovered:

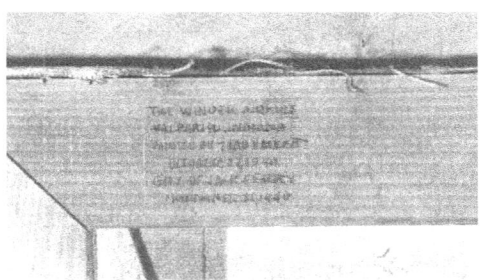

The Winder Airport
Valparaiso, Indiana
Painted by Thad Hackett
October 27, 1940
Gift of Jack Ferry
November 21, 1940

Back cover photo shows Urschel Field pilots in 1940 at a farewell party for Bud Winder who is seated in the first row second from the left. Next to him on the right are Alex Nogard and Olie Sundelin.